BAD
HISTORY

Also by Emma Marriott
I Used to Know That: History

BAD
HISTORY

HOW
WE GOT THE
PAST
WRONG

EMMA MARRIOTT

MICHAEL O'MARA BOOKS LIMITED

First published in Great Britain in 2011 by
Michael O'Mara Books Limited
9 Lion Yard
Tremadoc Road
London SW4 7NQ

A CIP catalogue record for this book is available
from the British Library.

Papers used by Michael O'Mara Books Limited are natural,
recyclable products made from wood grown in sustainable forests.
The manufacturing processes conform to the environmental
regulations of the country of origin.

ISBN: 978-1-84317-617-6 in hardback print format
ISBN: 978-1-84317-778-4 in Mobipocket format
ISBN: 978-1-84317-777-7 in EPub format

1 2 3 4 5 6 7 8 9 10

Cover design by Ana Bjezancevic
Designed and typeset by www.glensaville.com
Maps and technical drawings by David Woodroffe
Illustrations by Andrew Pinder
Printed and bound in Great Britain by Clays Ltd, St Ives plc

www.mombooks.com

CONTENTS

INTRODUCTION

'HISTORY IS A PACK OF LIES ABOUT EVENTS THAT NEVER HAPPENED TOLD BY PEOPLE WHO WEREN'T THERE.' GEORGE SANTAYANA

The chronicles of history are littered with myths and legends, misinformation, falsehoods, embellishment, wild exaggeration and a great deal of confusion. And this makes for an awful lot of bad history. As Mr Santayana says, the problem with history is that *we weren't actually there*, and we rely on other people who also weren't there to tell us what happened and why. This means that historical 'facts', like the ones drummed into us at school, are not quite what they seem: the best we can say for a lot of them is that they are 'probably true', whilst others – like Britain was once a fully integrated province of the Roman Empire or Mussolini made the trains run on time – turn out to be, well, probably not true.

There are a myriad of reasons why events or people from the past are misrepresented or misunderstood. Archaeological or documentary evidence may be lacking, unreliable or bewilderingly inconsistent (ask ten or twenty witnesses what happened at a particular incident and you'll get ten or twenty different versions). Extrapolating what happened at any given event is a tricky business: if you then add in a large chunk of time, be it a decade or several centuries, then some might say it's an almost impossible task.

Problems also arise when we wrench something out of the past and examine it out of context. We can't pretend we don't live in the present, and however much we try, modern sensibilities shape our view of history – and the conclusions that we draw often speak volumes about our own beliefs. In the last century, Cecil Rhodes was revered as a great Empire builder; now many think of him as a crook and an arrogant bully. Which is it to be? And which is the example of 'bad history'?

History, like life, is annoyingly complex (and confusing); so packaging the past into a neat argument so that it fits some kind of preconceived notion also has its dangers. We liken our historical figures to imaginary characters, and mould them into the comforting stereotypes of hero or rogue. We forget, however, that they were real-life people and, like us, were probably a combination of the good and bad. We much prefer our victories in battle to be resounding and decisive, and not, like many military engagements, muddled, open-ended and inconsequential affairs. Whilst these embellishments make for exciting stories – we all love a dashing hero or a thumping victory – they also distort the truth, endorse delusions of grandeur and perpetuate many of the myths with which we are so familiar.

Historical myths, like fairy tales, are generally quite harmless but when they are seized upon as political weaponry, the consequences can be disastrous. Repressive regimes can cover up a discreditable past or rewrite the history books with their own sanitized version of events (see Chairman Mao) and propagandists and political leaders can appropriate popular historical myths to lend authority to their own rather dubious belief system (see the Bismarck myth and Hitler). Conversely, some theorists who are hell-bent on proving some kind of government conspiracy or cover-up can also wander into rather dodgy territory (see the attack on Pearl Harbor).

What follows is an investigation into some of the myths and falsehoods that have become entrenched in popular belief and wrongly influenced our understanding of the world. It is by no means exhaustive – there are without a doubt many more myths out there – but I hope it goes some way to shedding light on some of the worst offences. Some will disagree with the findings – I too 'wasn't there' and, as the historian Pieter Geyl said (at least, I hope he said it), 'History is an argument without end'. But I'm hoping that the history passed down to us is not all a pack of lies, that lurking amongst all that bad history lies the truth – we just need to keep looking for it.

Emma Marriott

THE AMERICAN OLD WEST WAS A WILD AND DANGEROUS PLACE TO BE

Few areas of history have gripped the imagination as much as the expansion of the United States into the wilderness of the West. Sensational tales of the 'Wild West' portrayed a violent and brutal land where hardy settlers rubbed alongside brave cowboys, ruthless outlaws and savage Indians, where people took the law into their own hands to protect themselves and their families.

This image of the Old West proved hugely popular and was consolidated in American folklore, music and dime novels that were published in their millions in the latter half of the nineteenth century. Soldier and showman Buffalo Bill Cody similarly popularized the legend of the frontier land through his Wild West shows. Queen Victoria attended one of his shows at Earls Court in 1867 and wrote in her diary, 'an attack on a coach and on a ranch, with an immense deal of firing, was most exciting, so was the buffalo hunt, and the bucking ponies, that were almost impossible to sit …'

In the twentieth century, the legend of the Wild West spread to the rest of the world as artists, magazines and movies spun a whole industry around its mythologization, in which gun-slinging heroes battled against 'Injuns' in places where, as Sergio Leone put it, 'life has no value'. The first Western movie, *The Great Train Robbery*, came out in 1903 and by the 1950s the genre was also lapped up by US television audiences who by 1959 could choose from no fewer than twenty-six prime-time Western series.

Yet the reality of life in the West was quite different from the general lawlessness depicted in the movies. Recent research has shown that crime was relatively low among the West's settlers and you were more likely to be gunned down in Victorian London than in the Wild West. In the real Dodge City, which at one point was thought of as the biggest and rowdiest town of the Wild West, a total of five deaths in 1878 amounted to the town's worst year for homicides. Similarly, the legendary shoot-out at the OK Corral, a gunfight between two gangs led by Wyatt Earp and Ike Clanton (and regarded as the most famous gun battle in the history of the Old West) lasted all of sixty seconds and resulted in just three deaths. Face-offs at noon were not common events and gunfights were usually spontaneous and the result of drunken arguments that had got out of hand. The Wild West mythmakers would also have us believe that bank robberies were everyday events, but Larry Schweikart of the University of Dayton has estimated that between 1859 and 1900 just *twelve* bank robberies occurred along the Western frontier.

Research has also shown that, in the absence of any formal government, settlers devised surprisingly effective ways to protect themselves from all manner of crimes. Voluntary organizations in the form of 'wagon-train' governments were set up to police and protect the 300,000 pioneers travelling west to California and Oregon, whilst in the Midwest, land clubs and cattlemen associations settled disputes and enforced property rights. On the west coast, gold-mining districts set up legal systems that punished crimes against life and property. On the whole, miners avoided violence and abided by the rules of the district. Andrew Morriss of Case Western Reserve University writes, 'This amazing polyglot of men seeking rapid wealth, and with virtually no intention of building a lasting society, created a set of customary legal institutions which not only flourished in California but successfully adapted to conditions across the West.'

COWBOYS

Also central to the Wild West myth was the gun-slinging cowboy, the embodiment of the brave lone-rider, who, we're led to believe, overran the frontier land. In reality, farmers outnumbered cowboys in the West by about a *thousand* to one: there were (at the most) only 10,000 working cowboys, the majority of whom were either Hispanic, African American or Mexican. Few cowboys could afford a firearm (a modern Colt weapon represented an average nine months' salary) and many died young, not from shoot-outs but from riding accidents or illnesses borne from a hard but decidedly unglamorous life herding cows across vast plains.

Other old West myths, largely popularized by the entertainment industry, include the image of westward migrants lumbering across the Great Plains in Conestoga wagons (large wagons pulled by oxen). In fact, most families used much smaller covered wagons called 'prairie schooners', which were hauled by mules or oxen. In addition, wagon trails were not constantly assailed by Indians – most crossed the plains without incident; nor would trails of wagons defend themselves from attacking Indians by manoeuvring themselves into galloping circles (the movies borrowed this from the Wild West shows in which limited arena space necessitated the circular formation). Any killings by Indians tended to be wildly exaggerated: of the half a million people who passed through Indian territories in wagon trains between 1840 and 1860 it's estimated that just 362 died from attacks by hostile natives.

And yet, whilst bloodshed was relatively low amongst the West's new settlers, life for America's indigenous population was increasingly brutal. As migrants advanced west, Native Americans were uprooted and moved from their homelands, and many died as a result of war, disease or loss of livelihood. Between 1830 and 1895 the number of Native Americans fell from 2 million to 90,000, while around 70 million buffalo (the Plains Indians' main source of livelihood) were slaughtered. Hollywood has also given us a grossly distorted view of the Native American (see p.18).

The myth of the Wild West has captivated millions across the world and spawned a huge publishing and entertainment industry in the process. In the forging of the new nation of America, exaggerated tales of brave and hardy white men venturing into the unknown have proved far more appealing than the reality of the migrants' grittier, more mundane lives or the brutalities inflicted upon the West's indigenous population. This mythical depiction of the Wild West, perpetuated by Hollywood, was brilliantly satirized by Mel Brooks's 1974 film *Blazing Saddles*, none more so than in Sheriff Bart's farewell to the townspeople of Rock Ridge:

> *Bart: Work here is done. I'm needed elsewhere now. I'm needed wherever outlaws rule the West, wherever innocent women and children are afraid to walk the streets, wherever a man cannot live in simple dignity, wherever a people cry out for justice.*
>
> *Crowd: [in unison] BULLSHIT!*
>
> *Bart: All right, you caught me. Speaking the plain truth is getting pretty damn dull around here.*

I'd give you a belly full of lead, if only I could afford a gun.

THE NATIVE AMERICAN

Numerous myths surround Native Americans, who were caricatured in the Western movies either as dishonourable savages or, more recently, as a spiritual people who were at one with nature.

Native Americans did not greet each other with 'how'. Similarly, 'paleface' and 'Great White Father' were the invention of novelists like James Fenimore Cooper (*The Last of the Mohicans*). Indians did not send coded messages to other tribes via smoke signals, nor was scalping a common practice amongst them (but was actually introduced by the white settler). And the Native American showed as little concern for their environment as their white counterpart, reducing the population of beavers and the white-tailed deer to near extinction. The image of the Indian as the original environmentalist largely stems from a much-quoted 1854 speech by Chief Seattle, a Suquamish Indian whose words encapsulated the Indians' deeply spiritual kinship with nature, '... the earth does not belong to man – man belongs to the earth ...'

However, these words probably bear no relation to those actually spoken by Chief Seattle, as he delivered the speech in the Indian language of Lushootseed, which was simultaneously translated into Chinook Jargon. A Dr Henry Smith then reproduced the speech from memory in 1887, and various adaptations have appeared ever since.

HENRY V: 'THE GREATEST MAN THAT EVER RULED ENGLAND'

Henry V (reigned 1413-22) is regarded as a great English hero – a warrior king and deliverer of England who achieved a stunning victory at Agincourt in 1415. Shakespeare's depiction of Henry V as a dashing young king with a charismatic, cheerful personality and orator of great speeches built on and immortalized this iconic image of Henry. Similarly, Laurence Olivier's film *Henry V*, delivered with nationalist fervour during the Second World War, further consolidated Henry's image as the champion of England. And such admiration has extended to many historians, not least to K. B. McFarlane, who declared that Henry was 'the greatest man that ever ruled England'.

And yet this adoration is considered by some as an over-simplified approach that ignores the complexities and failings of this medieval king. Recent research, notably by the historian Ian Mortimer for his book *1415: Henry V's Year of Glory*, has revealed that Henry was in fact a dour 'militant Catholic fundamentalist … a deeply flawed individual … capable of great cruelty'. In short, Henry was not the charismatic, flamboyant hero as portrayed by propagandists and Shakespeare's *Henry V* but a severe, arrogant man and a ruthless killer.

During Henry's own lifetime, propagandists portrayed him as a heroic king who was divinely inspired to rule. And there was some truth to Henry's heroism. As a teenager he led his own army against Owain Glyndŵr in Wales and joined forces with his father Henry IV against Harry Hotspur at the Battle of Shrewsbury in 1403 (where he received a facial scar after an arrow pierced six inches below his right eye). Having witnessed rebellion and attempts on his father's life, Henry V knew his position as Lancastrian ruler was precarious and he therefore sought divine blessing for his kingship through military victory. Ever mindful of his dynastic position, Henry was also religious, even when compared to the religious piety of the time, and it was the powerful combination of ambition and religious fervour that drove his every move.

Early on in his reign, Henry founded new religious communities (mainly for the most zealous orders like the Carthusians) and he also helped to bring an end to the schism in the Roman Catholic Church (which had at one point three competing popes). He's also been credited as the first king to use the English language in his letters; however, Mortimer suggests that Edward III – who ensured the law courts used English – and Henry IV did more to promote the English language than Henry V did. Similarly, Churchill also spoke of Henry V as the founder of the English navy, whereas Edward III had a considerably larger navy at his disposal, although Henry was the first of the English monarchs to understand the role of the sea in conflict.

Much of Henry's early lawmaking and economic reforms were enforced with the specific intention of waging an aggressive war with France. His main aim was to win back the lost territories of France, unite the English and French kingdoms and in the process legitimize his rule through God-given victory. Whilst Henry's military campaigns in France showed a high degree of military planning and organization – and Henry himself exhibited courage and tenacity when he turned potential disaster into triumph at Agincourt in 1415 – Mortimer suggests that luck played a big part in Henry's military endeavours, particularly on the night of 24–25 October 1415 when heavy rain and mud made the ground too soft. This seriously debilitated the French army because it hampered their cavalry, making it impossible to charge, and ultimately led to English victory.

ARMIES AT AGINCOURT

Whilst the French army was bigger, historians have tended to exaggerate the ratio of French to English at Agincourt by as much as 7:1. Mortimer suggests it was actually more like 2:1 as the French army contained many more non-combatant pages than the English counterpart.

Panicked by the prospect of a second French attack, Henry then ordered a massacre by commanding his men to cut the throats of hundreds of prisoners (an ugly episode omitted by Shakespeare altogether). In breach of basic chivalric codes, Henry's slaughter included men of noble birth, and he was to show similar acts of great cruelty throughout his reign. At Caen in 1417, during Henry's subsequent conquest of Normandy, he ordered the killing of 1,800 men in cold blood. And at home, a contemporary Jean de Warin wrote that Henry 'punished with death without any mercy those who disobeyed or infringed his commands', whilst also actively pursuing the persecution of heretics. The followers of John Wycliffe, the Lollards, suffered most at the hands of Henry, to include his old battlefield friend Sir John Oldcastle whom Henry burnt to death early on in his reign. Although previous historians have argued that these persecutions were in keeping with the period, Ian Mortimer has noted that in the first year alone of Henry V's reign seven men were burnt alive, whereas no men were burnt for heresy under Edward III or Richard II, and just two men were executed for heresy by his father, Henry IV.

In the last five years of his reign, all but three months were spent in France, and his brothers – especially his eldest brother John, Duke of Bedford, who was appointed keeper of England during Henry's French campaign – and the court were responsible for many of his domestic achievements at home. Shakespeare and past accounts have played up Henry's 'individual' greatness, whereas the potential of his three brothers, John, Thomas and Humphrey, was completely overshadowed.

Henry's early death in 1422, during a siege in France, no doubt contributed to his semi-legendary status. But, in the main, it was his victory at Agincourt that led to his enduring image of greatness. 'We few, we happy few, we band of brothers' were the words that Shakespeare used to enshrine the national myth that the English do best when they are outnumbered. (A notion used to great effect several centuries later by Winston Churchill.) On the continent, however, Agincourt is remembered in quite a different way: as a battle that resulted in mass slaughter, at the behest of a merciless king who shamelessly betrayed the traditional rules of chivalry.

THE FOUNDING FATHERS OF THE US SOUGHT TO REPLACE MONARCHY WITH DEMOCRACY

The US Constitution, devised in 1787 in Philadelphia, established the foundation of the US government as we know it today; with the creation of the bicameral Congress (the House and Senate), the executive branch of the Presidency and the judicial arm of the Supreme Court. As the Constitution provided the framework for representative democracy in the US (a political system now ardently defended by Americans), it seems only reasonable to presume that the Founding Fathers, that is the men who framed the Constitution, intended to establish a nation based upon democratic principles.

In reality, the Founding Fathers – who included such luminaries as Benjamin Franklin and George Washington – were wholly united in their opposition to and mistrust of democracy. For them, and for many of their contemporaries, democracy equalled mob rule and anarchy, and the word itself had somewhat grubby associations. The fifty-five delegates who devised and worded the Constitution were largely members of the gentry and lawyers, and a third of them had served in Washington's army. Whilst showing a great deal of intellect and foresight, they shared a conservative outlook and were not shy in voicing their hostility towards democracy: Delegate Edmund Randolph spoke of the 'follies and turbulence of democracy', whilst Roger Sherman said that 'the people immediately should have as little to do as may be about the Government'.

Although the delegates favoured a government that represented the people – and the US franchise in the 1780s, whereby any white freeman of voting age could vote, was already very broad when compared to the rest of the world – their intention was to set up an administration where the people would be limited in how much they could directly participate in national government. Many of the Founding Fathers advocated strict limitations and checks on the 'democratic parts' of the Constitution and almost all of them envisioned a nation ruled by propertied gentlemen. At one stage, Delegate Alexander Hamilton suggested that the senate and president be elected for life and given absolute power over the states. And following George Washington's rather grand ceremonial inauguration, Congress actually considered altering his title to the more impressive-sounding 'His Highness', 'His Mightiness' or 'His Supremacy', until they backtracked to the more sober-sounding President.

In the end, the delegates made one concession to democracy when it was decided that the House of Representatives would be chosen by the people (the 'people' being white, male property owners). The Senate, however, would be elected by the state legislature, as would the presidency (and it wasn't until 1913 that senators could be elected by popular vote). The word democracy continued to be avoided decades after 1781: the Declaration of Independence omitted it and Thomas Jefferson as president didn't include the word in any public addresses. The 'Democratic' party discarded the word 'Republican' from its name only in 1844 and it wasn't until the twentieth century that US politicians generally referred to the US nation as a democracy (after Woodrow Wilson became the first president to do so in a public statement during the First World War).

Since the adoption of the Constitution, a further twenty-seven amendments have broadened the electorate and led to the democratization of US politics. These amendments have largely dismantled the limitations specifically incorporated by the Founding Fathers, whose ideas about political representation were mainly rooted in the colonial past. As delegate William Livingston put it, 'The people ever have been and ever will be unfit to retain the exercise of power in their own hands, they must of necessity delegate it somewhere.'

**His Mightiness
King George**

THE UNITED STATES OF GERMANY

It is frequently stated with conviction that Congress considered making German the official language of America, and that it was rejected by just one vote. This is, however, a myth as no such proposal was ever considered by any legislative body of the US government, particularly as around 90 per cent of the US's 3.9 million inhabitants spoke English. In 1795, the House of Representatives briefly considered a proposal that all laws and regulations be published in German *and* English (for the benefit of German citizens in the United States who could not speak English). It was never a popular motion and a vote to adjourn and sit again on the recommendation was rejected by one vote. A month later, it was again raised in the House of Representatives and was immediately and resoundingly rejected. The writer Kingsley Amis also claimed that Congress voted on establishing Ancient Greek as well as an American Indian language, the official language of America: again, not true.

The 'Iron Chancellor' Otto von Bismarck: Ruthless, War-Mongering Conservative and Dogmatic Ideologue

Prussian-born Otto von Bismarck is considered the founder of the German Empire, a man who from 1862 to 1890 shaped the fortunes of Germany, first as Minister-President of Prussia and then as Chancellor of the newly established German Empire. For decades after his death in 1898, Bismarck was venerated as a national hero, the 'most German of all Germans'. But when his image was used to legitimize the far-right politics that came to plague Germany in the 1930s and 1940s Bismarck's legacy took a real battering and led to the demonization of him as a ruthless, ultra-conservative despot, whose style paved the way for the Nazi regime.

Having achieved a series of Prussian victories in Europe, Bismarck secured in 1871 the political unification of German states and, with the European power balance radically altered, skilfully maintained peace through a series of European alliances. At home, the 'Iron Chancellor' set up a national currency and initiated a common code of German law, whilst implementing a number of laws designed to severely limit the influence of the Social Democratic Party and the Catholic Church.

Although always a staunch conservative and opponent of liberalism, Bismarck was not a dogmatic ideologue, nor was he fixated on war in Europe. Indeed, in foreign affairs, he developed into a master of diplomacy and the conduct of foreign affairs became one of his main preoccupations throughout his chancellorship. He purposely *avoided* war by maintaining an elaborate and constantly shifting system of political alliances in Europe that were aimed at isolating France (which remained a bitter enemy of Germany). At home, his aim was to build a powerful German Reich and develop a national consciousness, and while he attacked Catholicism and Socialism in pursuit of this, he did personally reject anti-Semitism and viewed radical nationalism as a threat to the peace and security of the German Empire.

After Bismarck's resignation in 1890 and death in 1898, conservatives and liberals alike mythologized him as a ruthless promoter of the policy of 'Blood and Iron' (referring to his speech of 1862): 'Not by speeches and majority decisions are the great questions of the day decided – that was the great error of 1848 and 1849 – but by iron and blood.' As Kaiser Wilhelm II's popularity declined during the 1920s, Bismarck was increasingly revered as the man who had laid the foundations of Germany's 'greatness', whose strong leadership contrasted sharply with the weakness of parliamentary rule. He was to become one of the most popular German statesmen of all time.

As Robert Gerwarth describes in *The Bismarck Myth*, the mythologization of Bizmarck proved a useful ideological tool for future German leaders and politicians, but it would eventually lead to the misappropriation of his image.

Kaiser Wilhelm II first utilized Bismarck's reputation to

A Complex Character

The crude stereotype of Bismarck as a 'power politician in soldier's boots' – as coined by Ulrich von Hassell, leading member of the German resistance movement against Hitler – bears little relation to his more complex character. Bismarck's appearance seemed to fit the indomitable image – with his thick moustache, stern eyes and bearing of a Prussian officer (he usually wore his uniform in public, although he had only a very inglorious year of military service, which he did not enjoy) – whereas his temperament seemed more artistic and highly strung, earning him the name of 'wild Bismarck' in his twenties. Later in life, he would often resort to tantrums and crying fits to get his way with his sovereign. His public speeches were not the rants of a megalomaniac but were carefully worded (they still read well today) and he delighted in using sarcasm and irony.

justify Germany's expansionist policies overseas (although Bismarck had originally opposed the acquisition of foreign colonies, considering them too expensive) whilst attacking those who opposed the social order of Germany as a crime against the legacy of the Iron Chancellor. After the First World War and the subsequent humiliation of the German state (that Bismarck had created), Bismarck served as a reminder of what

Germany had lost. Mounting dissatisfaction with the Weimer Republic along with the Great Depression after 1929 further intensified the desire for a strong and charismatic leader, a 'second Bismarck' who could solve Germany's problems and reassert its former greatness.

The adulation of Bismarck also gave an emerging style of right-wing politics a historical legitimacy. Adolf Hitler (although as an Austrian he was a 'self-elected' Prussian) evoked the memory of Bismarck and Frederick the Great, and presented himself as the only man able to continue their legacy, declaring in January 1931 that 'if Bismarck were to return with his political comrades, they would all stand on our side today'. However, once Hitler's regime was established in 1933, the public veneration of Bismarck faded, for the Nazis could not now allow the greatness of past leaders to overshadow that of Adolf Hitler. For this reason, as Robert Gerwarth in *History Today* noted, public Bismarck celebrations were declared illegal in Germany.

The mythologization of Bismarck (and its appropriation by future leaders) ultimately proved disastrous for Germany, although the vast disparities between Hitler, a reckless gambler and demagogue who brought ruin to Germany, and Bismarck, a cautious political player, but a gambler when he needed to be, are clear. In 1944, when Germany's total defeat was imminent, Ulrich von Hassell, who at one-time hadn't been Bismarck's greatest ally, lamented:

It is regrettable, what a false picture of him we ourselves have given the world – that of a power politician in soldier's boots – in our childish joy over the fact that at least someone had made Germany a name to reckon with again. In his own way he knew how to win confidence in the world; exactly the reverse of what is done today. In truth, the highest diplomacy and great moderation were his real gifts.

THE ADULATION OF BISMARCK

Bismarck received far more adulation after his resignation and death than he ever did as Chancellor. His shifting foreign policy and his anti-Catholicism and anti-Socialism created distrust within the political culture of Germany. However, he abandoned his anti-Catholic stance in the 1880s and, despite Bismarck, the Socialists continued to flourish so that by 1914 they were the biggest party in the Reichstag. The German press expressed little grief over Bismarck's resignation and his departure from Berlin was accompanied by cheering crowds. The novelist Theodor Fontane even wrote in a letter, 'it is good fortune that we finally got rid of him'.

Bolsheviks, Under the Charismatic Leadership of Lenin, Heroically Stormed the Winter Palace in the October Revolution of 1917

The October Revolution of 1917, which followed the February Revolution of the same year, saw the Bolsheviks seize power in Russia. Bolshevik Red Guards began the takeover of key buildings in Petrograd on the night of 24–25 October 1917 and finally captured the Winter Palace, the seat of Russia's Provisional Government, the following night. 'Official' histories, paintings, novels and films have depicted the storming of the Winter Palace as part of a mass rising, in which large numbers fought fiercely to break into a heavily guarded palace, yet the reality of the Revolution was far less dramatic.

Indeed, this depiction of events is, as the historian Steve Phillips puts it in *Lenin and the Russian Revolution*, 'a gross exaggeration'. Much of it is based on 'politically correct' accounts created by Bolshevik propagandists, whose intention was to portray the events of October 1917 as a heroic and dramatic struggle. This was reinforced by an official historical re-enactment shown to 100,000 spectators on the third anniversary of the Revolution. Entitled *The Storming of the Winter Palace* it depicted a huge siege and fierce battle. Later films portrayed a similar image, significantly Sergei Eisenstein's *October: Ten*

Days That Shook the World, a documentary-style movie made in 1927, which showed Bolshevik leader Lenin and thousands of Red Guards storming the palace. So authentic did this movie seem to be that for years television documentaries passed off this particular scene as actual 'footage' from the Revolution.

Free from official Soviet biases, Western historians have interpreted the Revolution in numerous ways, and many have debunked the heroic myth of a large-scale struggle. Indeed, the real events of October were far less dramatic: by the time the Bolsheviks entered the Winter Palace, it was virtually unoccupied; its gates were open, its administrative staff and many of its guards had fled, and the few that remained had barricaded themselves in the former private rooms of the Imperial Family. Kerensky's Provisional Government had by this time little support in the city and virtually no power, so much so that, as Steve Phillips remarks in *Lenin and the Russian Revolution*, 'it was hardly worth overthrowing'.

General Knox, a British military attaché in Russia, observed the taking of the palace:

The garrison of the Winter Palace originally consisted of about 2,000 all told … The garrison dwindled owing to desertions … No one had any stomach for fighting; and some of the ensigns even borrowed great coats of soldier pattern from any women to enable them to escape unobserved … At 10 p.m., a large part of the ensigns left, leaving few defenders except the ensigns of the Engineering School and the company of women. [The so-called Women's Death Battalions.]

The American-born journalist and Socialist John Reed also witnessed the siege and wrote in his book *Ten Days That Shook the World* (on which Eisenstein's film was based) that by 2 a.m., once Bolshevik insurgents had flooded into the building, 'there was no violence done although the Junkers were terrified'. Such was the mammoth and heroic storming of the symbol of Tsarism: the Winter Palace.

Cultural depictions of Vladimir Lenin and his role in the events of 17 October have also been misrepresented. Contrary to popular myth, he did not lead the Bolshevik troops into the palace, nor did he spur on the insurgents with a string of public speeches (as depicted in films, novels and even ballets with 'fist raised, mouth tensed and a bearded chin'). On that particular day, Lenin – who, incidentally, had no beard at this time in an attempt to disguise himself from the authorities – spoke only briefly at the Second Congress and acted more as a strategist and, as Robert Service notes in *Lenin*, an 'inspirer behind the scenes'.

It's estimated that only six people lost their lives in Petrograd during the October Revolution, of whom none were defenders of the existing government. Unlike the February Revolution – during which roughly 1,500 people died and hundreds of thousands were out on the streets protesting – this was not a mass rising. The Winter Palace was not 'stormed' by thousands of troops, but simply walked into by a much smaller group of fairly disorganized soldiers, who faced little or no opposition.

LEON TROTSKY

The military force needed to overthrow the Provisional Government in Petrograd was largely orchestrated by Leon Trotsky, not Lenin. Trotsky joined the Bolsheviks just prior to the October Revolution and, as chairman of the Soviet Petrograd (from 8 October), he set up the Military Revolutionary Committee, which took over the capital's garrison and city a week before the uprising, leaving just the Winter Palace holding out on the night of 24–25 October. On 10 November 1918, Stalin wrote in *Pravda*:

All practical work in connection with the organization of the uprising was done under the immediate direction of Comrade Trotsky, the President of the Petrograd Soviet. It can be stated with certainty that the Party is indebted primarily and principally to Comrade Trotsky for the rapid going over of the garrison to the side of the Soviet and the efficient manner in which the work of the Military Revolutionary Committee was organized.

A somewhat ironic statement considering Stalin would later hound and hunt Trotsky to his death.

Christopher Columbus Introduced Syphilis to Europe

It is a commonly held belief that the Italian explorer Christopher Columbus introduced syphilis to Europe. During his historic voyage to the Americas in 1492, it was thought that the Columbian crew had picked up the unfamiliar disease of syphilis from the Americas and brought it back to Europe the following year. However, recent discoveries have shown that syphilis may well have existed in Europe long before Columbus first set foot in the New World.

The theory of Columbus's culpability is not without foundation as the earliest-known European epidemic of syphilis broke out in 1494–5, soon after Columbus's return. The disease struck French troops in Naples during their invasion of Italy, and documentary evidence cites links between the French army and crewmen of the Columbus voyage. Syphilis went on to ravage Europe and led to an estimated 5 million deaths. In an era without antibiotics, it was a fearsome disease and caused serious damage to its victim's skin, joints, stomach, heart and brain, leading to death within a few months.

In 2008 the *New Scientist* magazine reported on new evidence of different strains of syphilis and related bacteria, which also supported the Columbian link. Findings indicated that the sexually transmitted form of syphilis originated recently, suggesting that Europeans could have picked up a non-venereal form of the disease, which then mutated into a more deadly, sexually transmittable form. Added to this, examinations of the venereal-causing strains of syphilis appeared to be closely related to those found in South America (where Columbus and his crew landed).

THE COLUMBIAN EXCHANGE

Columbus's voyage to the Americas in 1492 launched an era of wide-scale contact between the New and Old Worlds, known as 'The Columbian Exchange' (a term coined by the historian Alfred W. Crosby). New foodstuffs and crops (including tobacco), animals, ideas and people (often in the form of slaves) were exchanged, as were a host of deadly diseases. European afflictions, which included influenza and smallpox, decimated the population of the Americas and it has been estimated that between 1492 and 1650 the indigenous 'Indian' population of the Americas declined from 50 million to 5 million. Thus, for many people in the Americas, Columbus kick-started a rapid decline in population with genocidal effect.

However, recent evidence has established the existence of syphilis in Europe long before the voyage of 1492. In east London, on the site of one of the largest hospitals in the medieval period, osteologists like Brian Connell have unearthed skeletons dating from 1200 to 1400 that show clear signs of the syphilis disease. Out of 5,387 skeletons examined, a total of twenty-five show the terrible bone damage inflicted by the condition. One skeleton belonged to a ten-year-old child, who experts believe had been born with the infection, and whose remains showed the painful, disfiguring symptoms characteristic of its later stages: syphilitic lesions had caused dents in the child's skull and its canine teeth protruded at a forty-five-degree angle. Brian Connell said, 'It caused a bit of stir when it was found because the symptoms are so obvious.'

Recent discoveries in the ruins of Pompeii also indicate that syphilis was present in early Europe, as the remains of twin children who died in the eruption of Mount Vesuvius in AD 79 have been found to show almost certainly the signs of congenital (hereditary) syphilis. Some experts believe that Hippocrates described the symptoms of venereal syphilis in Ancient Greece. In addition, skeletons of monks who lived at a thirteenth- to fourteenth-century Augustinian friary in Kingston-upon-Hull in England showed bone lesions indicative of venereal syphilis. Douglas Owsley, an anthropologist at the Smithsonian Institution, also put forward the idea that syphilis had existed in both hemispheres but was mistaken in the medieval period for leprosy – it is simply coincidental that the mistaken leprosy symptoms flared up in virulence at the end of the fifteenth century. Other molecular geneticists have argued that it's likely syphilis emerged in Europe spontaneously, possibly from related bacteria already rife in the Old World.

Although the first known European epidemic of syphilis broke

The Columbus Myth

Columbus was once thought of as the 'discoverer' of America, even though the indigenous people had been there for thousands of years and the Vikings had settled there several centuries earlier. What also tends to be forgotten is that Columbus never actually set foot in North America as his four voyages took him to the Caribbean and the coast of South America. Added to that, when he first reached Cuba, he insisted that it was part of the Asian mainland and thus named its inhabitants 'indios' (leaving us 'Indians').

For almost three hundred years after his voyages Columbus was largely forgotten, until post-revolutionary Americans, in their search for heroes unconnected with the British monarchy, resurrected his memory and mythologized his life in institutions, regions, books and song (the lyrics to 'Hail Columbia' date from 1798). In the 1930s President Franklin D. Roosevelt (partly in a bid to please Italian Americans, who were important supporters of his party) revived the myth and established the Columbus Day public holiday. The spirit of Columbus ran through all Americans, Roosevelt maintained: 'You are scarcely removed one generation from men and women who [...] sought to conquer nature for the benefit of the Nation.'

out in the immediate aftermath of Columbus's historic voyage, he was not responsible for bringing the disease to Europe. New evidence suggests syphilis had been present in Europe as early as the first century AD, and therefore the man who was once credited as being the first European to reach the Americas (another case of 'bad history' – see p.39) – and who may have instigated the exchange of a host of other diseases between the Old and New Worlds (see p.37) – has finally been exonerated.

The Main Killing Sites of the Holocaust were Auschwitz and the Concentration Camps in Germany

For many in Western Europe, the image of the Holocaust centres upon Auschwitz and the German concentration camps. These were seen as the main killing sites of the Jews in Europe – mass murder achieved on an industrial scale, largely by means of the gas chamber. Memoirs, photographs, news footage and novels portray the appalling images with which we are now familiar, and these now stand as testament to one of the worst atrocities of the twentieth century.

The Camps

The term 'concentration camp' has been used synonymously for all types of camps established by Nazi Germany but there was a distinct difference between the concentration camp and the extermination camp. The former were set up as places of incarceration, and the latter were established for the sole purpose of industrial-scale mass murder. As Timothy Snyder in his groundbreaking book *Blood Lands* writes, 'The concentration camps did kill hundreds of thousands of people at the end of the war, but they were not (in contrast to the death facilities) designed for mass killing.'

Nazi death and concentration camps

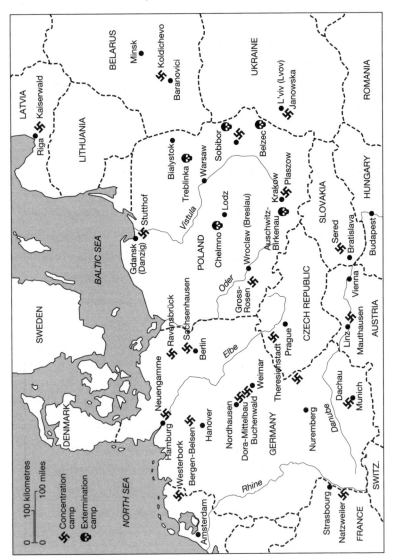

Auschwitz was built in German-occupied Poland and served as both a concentration camp and an extermination camp (located in nearby Birkenau). It became Nazi Germany's main extermination site by 1944, and approximately one sixth of the 5.7 million Jews killed in the Holocaust died there from February 1943 onwards. And yet Auschwitz and the German concentration camps formed just one aspect of an appallingly intricate network of camps and directives designed by the Nazis to exterminate the European Jewish population, and others that they deemed unfit for life. As Snyder writes, 'Mass killing in Europe is usually associated with the Holocaust, and the Holocaust with rapid industrial killing. The image is too simple and clean.' In reality, the Germans utilized a host of other primitive methods of killing across German-occupied lands (and much of it outside of the extermination camps), from starvation and forced labour to impromptu executions and mass shootings.

Auschwitz

By 1944 Auschwitz had become the main site of the Holocaust because the Germans had been forced out of the Soviet Union and were unable to continue their mass shootings of Soviet Jews. The approaching Red Army had also led to the closure of the Reinhard death camps in Poland.

The German occupation of Poland in 1939 swelled the number of Jewish people under Nazi control from around 300,000 (200,000 of which were German Jews, just 1 per cent of the German population) to around 2 million. After invasion, Polish civilians (Jewish and non-Jewish alike) were shot in their thousands by special squads called Einsatzgruppen, and from 1940 ghettos were set up as a form of holding pen and labour camp for the Jewish population until they could be deported elsewhere. More than 100,000 Jews were moved into the Warsaw ghetto in 1940, and around 60,000 died there as a result of starvation or deprivation.

Once Germany gained control of the Baltic States and the western Soviet Union in 1941, a total of some 5 million Jewish people came under the control of the Reich. In the same year Hitler gave Himmler and Goering the order to exterminate all Jews, and by August 1941 mass shootings in areas east of the Molotov-Ribbentrop Line (mainly eastern Poland, Lithuania, Latvia, Estonia and the western Soviet States, see map p.45) escalated to horrific proportions. The Einsatzgruppen, often enlisting local policemen and officials, oversaw many of the shootings and further SS reinforcements were sent in so that entire communities of men, women and children could be annihilated. In September 1941, as an act of reprisal for a bombing that had killed occupying Germans in Kiev, all Jews were ordered to appear at a certain point in the city, having been given the standard lie that they were to be resettled. Instead, they were driven to the edge of the Babi Yar ravine and shot, each person ordered to lie down on the long line of mounting corpses before they themselves were gunned down. The whole process took thirty-six hours and 33,761 people lost their lives. By the end of 1941, around a million Jews had been killed in this manner.

Mass shooting of civilians continued throughout 1942, and gas vans, first tested on Soviet POWs, were also utilized throughout German-occupied lands. West of the Molotov-Ribbentrop Line, gassing facilities were implemented and in Poland the extermination camps of Bełżec, Sobibor and Treblinka were set up. These relatively unknown camps, established to fulfil the Reinhard Action (named after Reinhard Heydrich, a Gestapo chief), were built purely for the purposes of murder (and were thus distinct from German concentration camps, such as Belsen and Dachau, which were designed primarily for slave labour and incarceration). Together with Chelmno, the Reinhard death camps went on to kill around 1.5 million Jews.

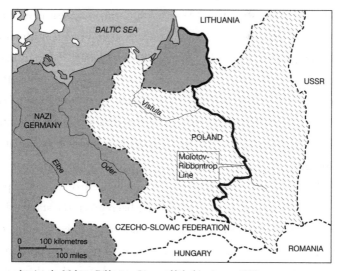

A map showing the Molotov-Ribbentrop Line established in August 1939

Whereas around 100,000 people survived Auschwitz, virtually no one who entered the death camps of Bełżec, Sobibor or Treblinka came out alive. The survivors of Auschwitz lived to speak of the horror of their experiences, whereas few people even knew of the existence of the Reinhard death camps because so few inmates survived. At the end of the war, American and British forces liberated German concentration camps, but they did not visit or witness the death facilities of Poland (some of which were liberated by the Red Army; others, including Bełżec, Sobibor and Treblinka, were demolished by the Nazis). Thus little was known about some of the Reinhard extermination camps, despite the huge numbers killed there (434,508 Jews were killed at Bełżec alone).

While Auschwitz was a major site of the Holocaust, by the time it had been set up, three-quarters of the Jews killed (and almost all of the biggest Jewish communities: the Polish and Soviet Jews) had already died. The majority of Jews killed didn't see a concentration camp and the atrocities committed in Auschwitz and the concentration camps of Nazi Germany did not represent the full horror of the Holocaust. In reality, the main killing sites were to be found in the extermination camps and across German-occupied lands, where civilians were slaughtered in their millions.

THE REALITY OF AUSCHWITZ

Most Jews who arrived at Auschwitz were gassed immediately. A minority were selected for labour and worked to exhaustion before being gassed. In addition, some 200,000 of Auschwitz's victims were not Jews – 74,000 being non-Jewish Poles and 15,000 were Soviets.

Only at Auschwitz were all inmates tattooed with an identification number. Formerly, inmates had had their numbers sewn into their clothes and they could be shot if they didn't remember their number. The tattooing practice began in spring 1943, by use of a large metal stamp comprising several needles forced into the upper left chest. From 1944, numbers were tattooed on to the left forearm.

Benito Mussolini Made the Trains Run on Time

'At least the trains ran on time under Mussolini': a statement frequently uttered by exasperated commuters or those trying to make the point that even brutal dictators have their good points. Unfortunately, they've fallen for Fascist propaganda, as Mussolini didn't make the trains run on time (nor did he have many good points).

The Italian rail network had fallen into a parlous state during the First World War and improvements were made to it in the 1920s and 1930s with the electrification of lines, the enhancement of rolling stock and the building of main routes between Rome and Naples, and between Bologna and Florence (which included the building of the second-longest tunnel in the world, opened with triumphant fanfare as 'building Fascism'). Peter Neville in *Mussolini,* however, maintains that much of the groundwork had already been put in place by the time Mussolini came to power. Mussolini's government benefited from recently established stock and relatively uncongested lines, and simply took the credit for many improvements initiated by previous administrations.

In 1936, American journalist George Seldes wrote that the trains more commonly used by tourists on the main express lines usually arrived on time but those on smaller lines were frequently late. Other testimonies from the period suggest that even the trains on the bigger lines were often delayed. The

British journalist Elizabeth Wiskemann dismissed the 'myth about the punctual trains ... I travelled in a number that were late,' she wrote.

THE ORIGINS OF EFFICIENCY

Mussolini came to power after the 'March on Rome' (which itself was a myth of Fascist propaganda) in 1922. Thereon, in a bid to win the Italian public over, he drew attention to the myth of Fascist efficiency, using the Italian train services as its symbol. Addressing a stationmaster, he is quoted as saying, 'We must leave exactly on time ... From now on everything must function to perfection.' Word soon spread that Mussolini had turned Italy's dilapidated old railway system into one that was the envy of the world. Infanta Eulalia of Spain wrote in her 1925 book *Courts and Countries After the War*, 'The first benefit of Benito Mussolini's direction in Italy begins to be felt when one crosses the Italian frontier and hears *"Il treno arriva orario."*' (The train is arriving on time.)

The notion that Italy's trains ran on time was largely created by the propaganda machine set up by the Fascist authorities. Mussolini's key priority in government was to subjugate the hearts and minds of the Italian people, and to impress on them and the wider world the benefits of Fascism versus the doctrines of liberalism or democracy. Press, radio, films and educational programmes went into overdrive as the new government pushed through various initiatives, often dubbing reforms as 'battles' (such as the marsh reclamation project, which was hailed as the 'Battle for Land'). In the same way, Mussolini used the rail industry to illustrate the effectiveness of his supposedly dynamic rule over everyday Italian life. George Seldes wrote, 'Official press agents and official philosophers … explained to the world that the running of trains was the symbol of the restoration of law and order.' The new government also took care to ban the reporting of all railway accidents and delays, thereby cementing the myth of train punctuality.

This myth has outstanding durability, largely because it seems to illustrate how something good can come out of the very worst circumstances. It was a view that similarly infuriated George Seldes, who complained in 1936 about fellow countrymen holidaying in Italy who when they returned to the US seemed to cry in unison, 'Great is the Duce, the trains now run on time.' And no matter how often they were told about Fascist oppression, injustice and cruelty, they always said the same thing: 'But the trains run on time.'

The Defeat of the Spanish Armada Was a Heroic Victory for the English and Marked the Beginning of England's Supremacy of the Seas

In 1588, the vast fleet of the Spanish Armada set sail for England. At the behest of its Catholic king, Philip II, the Spanish convoy aimed to invade England, remove Elizabeth I from the throne and thereby put an end to her piratical raids on Spanish ships and support of Protestant rebels in the Spanish-controlled Netherlands. A heroic battle ensued in which a smaller but more nimble convoy of English ships hounded and outwitted the huge Spanish fleet, eventually forcing it up the east coast of England and into the Atlantic Ocean.

The defeat of the Spanish Armada has generated a great deal of myth and confusion, much of it borne from the common perception that the battle represented a 'stunning underdog' victory for the English, who were vastly 'outnumbered and outgunned' by the Spanish fleet. In fact, the English had a greater number of better-equipped vessels in the water than the invading fleet, and had the erratic British weather, amongst other things, on their side.

As the Spanish Armada lay moored off Calais, unable to regroup with additional forces from the Low Countries, on the night of the 7 August the English set fire to several old ships and sent them crashing into the Spanish fleet.

A NUMBERS GAME

The Spanish fleet consisted of about 130 ships, most of which were troop-carrying vessels bearing 19,000 infantrymen under the command of the inexperienced Duke of Medina Sidonia. A minority of the Spanish ships, perhaps as few as thirty-five, were designed for warfare, with only nineteen of these fighting ships suited to the Atlantic waters. Whilst the Spanish had bigger, bulkier ships, the English confronted its adversary with a greater number of vessels, which were smaller but more nimble and easier to manoeuvre.

In the ensuing Battle of Gravelines, the English gained the upper hand, largely by means of cannon that could fire at long distances and rapidly reload when closer in. The English lost no ships, whereas it's frequently claimed the Spanish fleet suffered severe damage – in reality they lost just three ships, the seaworthiness of which was probably already in question. Lack of ammunition and worsening weather forced the English fleet to break off hostilities and the Armada was able to escape, in historian Felipe Fernández-Armesto's words, 'essentially intact and effectively undefeated, scotched but not killed, bloodied but unbowed'.

Strong winds then forced Medina Sidonia to order the Armada – still at this point a formidable fleet of ships, capable of sea warfare – to return to Spain and Portugal via the tip of

Scotland and Ireland. Storms – not English cannon – led to the sinking of numerous Spanish vessels as severe gales pushed them on to the rocky coasts of Scotland and Ireland. Whilst it was once thought that the majority of the Spanish fleet were lost in the Atlantic waters, Fernández-Armesto maintains that only twenty-one ships were sunk and up to five-sixths of the Spanish convoy returned home, with most of the main fighting ships intact.

The events of 1588 were almost immediately mythologized by English writers, who likened the repulse of the Spanish navy as the greatest English victory since Agincourt (see pages 19-22). The battle came to grip the national consciousness, whilst seeming to give strength to the Protestant cause in Europe. God himself had favoured what was seen as a moral English victory over the spiritually degenerate Spanish, and commemorative medals were issued, one with the inscription, 'He blew with His winds, and they were scattered'. The scale of the English victory was monumentalized as a battle of David and Goliath proportions when, as early as the summer of 1588, Thomas Deloney penned three ballads that described the Spanish fleet as having 'great Galleazzo,/which was so huge and hye' compared to the 'little Barkes' of the English. This depiction of the battle actually grew in potency so that even today the disparity between the might of the Spanish and English fleets is often overemphasized.

It's also commonly believed that the 1588 victory over the Spanish Armada saw the beginning of England's dominance over the seas. What tends to be forgotten is that the defeat of the Spanish Armada was just one of many sea and land battles fought during the Anglo-Spanish War between 1585 and 1604. Spain recovered quickly from the 1588 confrontation, rebuilt and retooled its navy (making subsequent vessels more nimble and effective) and defeated England in several military and naval engagements over the next decade. In 1588 an English Armada launched against the Spanish navy in 1589 resulted in total failure and heavy English casualties. In 1596 and 1597 Spain launched more Armadas against the English but adverse weather conditions continued to protect the British Isles from invasion. The Anglo-Spanish war ended in a stalemate but Spanish possessions in Europe and the Americas remained intact whilst efficient convoys of Spanish ships safeguarded and even expanded its lucrative trade route of precious metals from the Americas. Spain's victories at sea continued and were not seriously reversed until the 1630s, whereas England's maritime strength grew slowly and haltingly. By the late 1600s the Dutch overtook Spain as the leading sea power, and it wasn't until the mid-1700s that England truly ruled the waves.

The defeat of the Spanish Armada was in no way decisive, except in myth, and the size of the Spanish fleet and its losses are often vastly exaggerated. In the decade following 1588, Spain strengthened its navy and bolstered its overseas possessions, whereas England failed to capitalize on her early victory, had at this point no real foothold in the Americas and was again saved by the adverse weather – or 'Protestant wind' – of the Atlantic waters, which scuppered subsequent Spanish invasion.

CAPTAIN SCOTT: INTREPID ANTARCTIC EXPLORER AND ICONIC BRITISH HERO

British Antarctic explorer Captain Robert Falcon Scott, once seen as the quintessential British hero beloved of schoolboys across the land, has become the subject of bitter controversy. His iconic status as intrepid explorer, whose story captured the public's imagination for some sixty years after his death in 1912, came under sustained attack in the 1970s when closer examination of his polar expedition revealed that he was in fact a 'heroic bungler' who had led his comrades to their deaths.

Captain Scott's ill-fated Terra Nova Expedition into the Antarctic set off in 1910 with the expressed objective to 'reach the South Pole, and to secure for the British Empire the honour of this achievement'. On 17 January 1912, Scott and his four companions reached the South Pole only to discover that a Norwegian party led by Roald Amundsen had preceded them just under five weeks earlier. The 850-mile return journey – which Scott feared would be 'dreadfully tiring and monotonous' – ended in disaster as one by one the team perished from a combination of frostbite, starvation and exhaustion, with Scott himself probably dying last on or around 29 March 1912.

The frozen bodies of Scott and two other members of the team were discovered the following November, along with Scott's own letters and journals in which he had provided a powerful and harrowing account of the doomed expedition. Scott described how Captain Oates, with his leg frostbitten and gangrenous, uttered the immortal words, 'I am just going outside and may be some time,' before walking into a blizzard and certain death.

News of Scott and his men's deaths, combined with a memorial service in St Paul's Cathedral and the publication of his diaries at the end of 1913, had a huge impact on the British public. Although there was little interest in Scott before he left for the Antarctic (Shackleton was the preferred hero of the time), reports of his demise led to an immense outpouring of public grief as newspapers ran glowing tributes, and over the next dozen years monuments and memorials were set up around the country. The expedition of Scott – a story driven by the virtues of endurance, stoicism and suffering – aroused a strong nationalist spirit in the British people. The passing of the First World War served to increase the desire for a national hero and the 1922 publication of *The Worst Journey in the World* by Apsley Cherry-Garrard (one of the team who had discovered the bodies of Scott and his two companions) kept the memory of Scott alive. The 1948 film release of *Scott of the Antarctic*, in which Sir John Mills portrays Scott as a classic, stiff-upper-lipped hero, further established his legendary status for years to come.

A 'MESSAGE TO THE PUBLIC'

Scott's records also included a 'Message to the Public', written primarily as a defence of the team's actions, and which ended with the rousing words:

Had we lived, I should have had a tale to tell of the hardihood, endurance and courage of my companions which would have stirred the heart of every Englishman. These rough notes and our dead bodies must tell the tale, but surely, surely, a great rich country like ours will see that those who are dependent on us are properly provided for.

In 1979, however, Scott's heroic standing came under serious scrutiny with the publication of Roland Huntford's book *Scott and Amundsen*. Having examined in detail records from both the British and Norwegian expeditions, Huntford showed how Scott had failed in even the most basic principles of polar expedition. Not only did his lack of food supplies lead to the dehydration and malnutrition of the team, his equipment was inappropriate for the extreme weather. Whilst Amundsen's use of skis and ski champions, dogs (over 200 and with expert dog drivers) and sledges was an efficient combination, Scott's use of skis, dogs (just thirty-five), ponies (which were unsuited to the extreme weather), sledges and man-hauling (which Scott believed was less cruel than using animals, and somehow more noble) ultimately led to the deaths of all five men. Huntford saw a man who was disorganized, inflexible, over-sentimental and self-absorbed. The hero was toppled.

THE BENEFITS OF FUR

The Norwegian team was much better prepared for the extreme weather of the Antarctic. Amundsen had learnt from the Eskimos on the North-West Passage, using fur clothing and loose-fitting inner and outer garments to create air pockets and better air circulation. The British team shunned the use of fur, and instead used anoraks with separate hoods (fur was not deemed acceptable for civilized men due to its association with primitive tribes).

Later writers have sought to rescue Scott's reputation, in particular the polar explorer Sir Ranulph Fiennes who in his 2003 book *Captain Scott* vehemently dismissed Huntford's findings and described Scott as a great historic hero. Susan Solomon, in her research of the meteorological data in 1912, also put forward the theory that extreme weather conditions were to blame for Scott's failure. However Huntford's latest book *Race for the South Pole: The Expedition Diaries of Scott and Amundsen* contains the unedited diaries of Scott, with previous cuts, which had been carefully excised from earlier editions, restored. These complete journals show that Scott recognized early on that his preparations for the expedition were insufficient, that he blamed his colleagues for his own shortcomings and that, having discovered that Amundsen had reached the Pole before him, he clung to the hope that he could get home fast and 'get the news through first'. Also included (and translated for the first time into English) are Amundsen's and his team companion Olav Bjaaland's journals, which run parallel to Scott's and highlight the relative pace and position of the two expeditions on a daily basis. On a day when the Norwegian team covers fifteen miles in six and a half hours (Amundsen cheerfully describing it as 'our best day up here'), Scott's team is exhausted having man-hauled for eleven hours, covering just four miles (Scott describing it as 'a most damnably dismal day'). On another day, a blizzard forces the British team to shelter in their tent, whereas the Norwegians push on regardless. The comparisons between the two team-leaders are that of a professional explorer with that of a plucky but misguided amateur.

Having exhausted much of the evidence there is on the expedition, some would say Huntford has more or less laid the Scott myth to rest (although the controversy around it rages on). Scott's elevation to heroic status probably says more about the British psyche than anything else: his popularity soared after the First World War when the country yearned for a hero around which they could unite. Had he lived he probably would have been forgotten. Instead, his failure and subsequent death bestowed upon him a kind of untouchable nobility and the British 'have a perverse attraction to romantic heroes who fail rather than to Homeric ones who succeed'. The backlash against Scott simply reflected a cultural shift in Britain when the heroism he represented – a kind of mindless gallantry – was no longer held in such high regard.

A Heavy Load

When Scott's sledge was dug out, a geological collection weighing about twenty kilograms was discovered. Commander of the Terra Nova expedition ship Edward Evans wrote, 'It seems to me extraordinary that … they stuck to their specimens. We dumped ours at the first big check … I considered the safety of my party before the value of the records … apparently Scott did not.'

FRENCH REVOLUTIONARY DOCTOR JOSEPH GUILLOTIN INVENTED THE GUILLOTINE

The 'humane' decapitation machine known as the guillotine has long been associated with the bloody events of the French Revolution. Adopted by the National Assembly in 1791, the guillotine became the main official method of execution during the Revolution's Reign of Terror from September 1793 to July 1794, beheading the likes of Louis XVI, Marie Antoinette and Robespierre, along with thousands of other more ordinary French citizens. It's commonly assumed that the guillotine's namesake, Doctor Joseph-Ignace Guillotin, a French physician and secretary to the National Constituent Assembly in France, invented the mechanism.

However, the guillotine, or at least similar decapitation machines, predates the French Revolution by several centuries. Records dating back to *c.* 1286 show that a similar device known as the Halifax gibbet was used for executions in the market place of Halifax in West Yorkshire, England. A machine similar to the French guillotine can also be seen in a sixteenth-century engraving entitled *The execution of Murcod Ballagh near to Merton in Ireland 1307*, and in Scotland the Maiden, a machine based on the Halifax gibbet, was used for execution from the mid-sixteenth century onwards, as was the Italian *mannaia*. A German mechanism known as *fallbeil* (falling axe) was also used in various

German states from the seventeenth century onwards.

A Popular Method of Execution

The guillotine remained the official method of execution in France until the death penalty was abolished in 1981. The last guillotining occurred in 1977, with the last public execution (outside what is now the Palais de Justice, near Versailles) in 1939. The guillotine, along with firing squads, was also adopted as the official method of execution by both the German Empire and the Weimar Republic. Adolf Hitler adopted the mechanism and between 1933 and 1945 about 16,500 people were executed by guillotine in Germany and Austria.

Dr Joseph Guillotin, therefore, did not invent the device, he simply proposed to the Legislative Assembly in 1789 that this fairly common method of decapitation should become the sole method of execution in France. Opposition to traditional forms of execution – such as hanging, burning and beheading by sword or axe (hitherto reserved only for the rich and powerful) – had been growing in France, due mainly to the philosophies of the Enlightenment, which argued for a more humanitarian approach to execution, irrespective of the rank or status of the guilty party. Dr Guillotin's description of the machine – 'This mechanism falls like thunder; the head flies off, blood spurts, the man is no more' – was, according to some accounts, met with nervous laughter, and was at first rejected by the Assembly. It wasn't until 1791 that the Assembly agreed to its use, having been convinced of its effectiveness in causing an instant and humane death, decreeing that 'every person condemned to the death penalty shall have his head severed'.

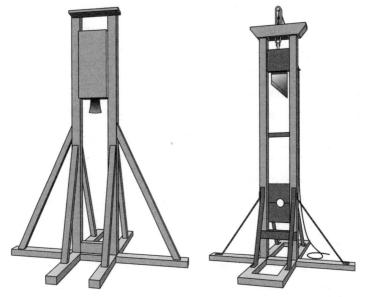

(L) The Halifax gibbet and (R) Schmidt's guillotine with its bevelled-edged triangular blade

By this point the initiative had passed from Dr Guillotin to Dr Antoine Louis, the secretary of the Academy of Surgeons. A German harpsichord-maker and engineer, Tobias Schmidt, built the first prototype and tested it on animals as well as some stocky human corpses from the hospital of Bicêtre, before the Assembly approved Schmidt's revised model (which changed the curved blade of the original device to a bevelled–edged triangular blade). The first execution took place on 25 April 1792, when the highwayman Nicolas Pelletier was beheaded on the Place de Grève.

WITHOUT DISCRIMINATION

It's commonly believed that the vast majority of the guillotine's victims were members of the aristocracy. In fact, 85 per cent of those killed by the guillotine were commoners, with some 1,200 members of the nobility beheaded by the device.

Copies of Schmidt's guillotine were sent out beyond Paris to all of France's new départements and there was to be no local variation. Originally known as the *louison* or *louisette*, after Antoine Louis, the name gradually evolved into the more familiar 'guillotine'. The macabre image of the device – its ruthless efficiency, the clean sweep of its blade followed by great pools of blood – transfixed France and Europe, spawning a host of nicknames, such as 'Madame Guillotine', and 'the national razor'.

During the Terror, the Revolution's bloodiest phase, thousands were sent to the guillotine. By 1795, over 1,000 people in Paris alone had been beheaded and by the end of the Revolution in 1799 some 16,000 people across France had been killed by decapitation. And yet, of the estimated 30,000 that died during the Terror the vast majority were not guillotined. Many were shot, drowned or beaten to death by mobs, as in Lyon on 4–8 December 1793 when people were lined up in front of open graves and shot by cannon.

Despite this, the guillotine became the pre-eminent symbol of the Revolution's Terror – the swift and brutal dispenser of justice. Although the Revolution broke new ground as, for the first time, the guillotine was unilaterally adopted across France as an official means of execution, it wasn't in itself a new invention, but a refinement of a device that had been in operation hundreds of years before Dr Guillotin was even born.

Dr Guillotin

Other myths purport that Dr Guillotin was himself beheaded by the machine that bears his name. He in fact lived to the ripe old age of seventy-six – he was briefly imprisoned towards the end of the Reign of Terror but was released in 1794 after Robespierre fell from power. His family petitioned the French government to rename the guillotine, in a bid to dissociate themselves from the butchery of the Terror. When the government refused, the Guillotin family changed their surname.

THE MAN IN THE IRON MASK WAS LOUIS XIV'S BROTHER

The Man in the Iron Mask was the name given to a French prisoner who was held in custody between 1669 and 1703 during the reign of King Louis XIV (1643–1715). Imprisoned in various French jails, it was said his face was always covered either by a black velvet cloth or an iron mask, and that he was guarded by two men ready to kill him should he remove his disguise. The identity of the enigmatic figure was never revealed and has been the focus of fierce debate (and romantic speculation) ever since.

He's been very quiet these past few days.
I think his jaw hinge has rusted up again!

The legend of the masked prisoner has spawned countless novels and films, most famously the third instalment of Alexandre Dumas's 1850 saga *The Three Musketeers*. And yet, whilst the story of the Man in the Iron Mask might seem like pure fabrication, documentary evidence, in the form of correspondence between prison and government officials, shows that the tale has some truth. The mysterious prisoner, originally named by the authorities as Eustache Dauger, was first imprisoned in 1669 at the fortress of Pignerol in Piedmont under the governorship of Bénigne Dauvergne de Saint-Mars. Louis XIV's war minister the Marquis de Louvois had previously written to Saint-Mars informing him of the arrival of the prisoner, who should be securely guarded and threatened with death should he speak of anything other than his most immediate needs. The letter and the circumstances surrounding his captivity suggest that this man was no ordinary prisoner and someone who obviously possessed information that posed a real threat to the security of the realm or to Louvois himself.

Saint-Mars subsequently took him to two other French prisons and finally in 1698 to the Bastille in Paris, where an officer of the prison, Lieutenant Etienne du Junca, wrote that Saint-Mars 'brought with him, in a litter, a longtime prisoner, whom he had in custody in Pignerol, and whom he kept always masked, and whose name has not been given to me, nor recorded.' In 1703 the prisoner reportedly died and was buried under the name of 'Marchioly'. Du Junca noted his death, referring to the deceased as 'the unknown prisoner who has worn a black velvet mask since his arrival in 1698'. Du Junca never referred to an iron mask, nor does any other reliable contemporary source mention one.

THE SKELETON IN THE CLOSET

The myth of the iron mask took on symbolic importance during the upheavals of the French Revolution. The masked prisoner, incarcerated for unknown reasons for thirty years, symbolized the tyranny and repression of an increasingly unpopular monarchy. When the Bastille was stormed in 1789, rumours circulated (and rumour it remained) that a skeleton was found hidden in the bowels of the prison, chained to a wall with an iron mask attached.

It was the writer and philosopher Voltaire who first claimed that the prisoner wore an iron mask – 'a movable, hinged lower jaw held in place by springs' – in his *Questions sur L'Encyclopédie*, published some time between 1770 and 1772. In this first historical account of the Man in the Iron Mask, Voltaire (amongst others) also claimed that the prisoner was the older, illegitimate brother of Louis XIV (son of Queen Anne of Austria, his mother, but not of Louis XIII) which would therefore have complicated the line of succession. A prisoner of royal descent would have explained the extraordinary circumstances surrounding his captivity, to include the need to conceal his identity and the reverence by which his jailers apparently treated him. This theory, however, presumes that Cardinal Mazarin (Richelieu's successor) had fathered a child with Queen Anne, and, while the two were close, there's no evidence to suggest any sexual impropriety between them.

THE MYTH CONTINUED …

Among other more fanciful suggestions, it was even rumoured (admittedly about a century after the Man in the Iron Mask's imprisonment) that the prisoner was the king's older brother, who had then fathered a child during his incarceration. The child had been sent to Corsica to be taken in by the Bonaparte family, which conveniently made Napoleon Bonaparte a direct descendent of the king. An appealing and fanciful notion, but no evidence exists to suggest it could actually be true.

The brother theme also proved popular with Dumas and various Hollywood filmmakers (including Leonardo DiCaprio's 1998 film *The Man in the Iron Mask*) who proposed that the prisoner was the identical twin brother of Louis XIV, whose birth had been hidden, then raised secretly away from court, and who then returned to claim his inheritance, leading to his imprisonment. A mask would have seemed a sensible precaution for a prisoner that bore a striking resemblance to the king. And yet no documentary evidence supports this theory and one can only presume it would have been impossible for the queen to conceal the birth and upbringing of a 'secret' twin brother.

As speculation to the identity of the masked prisoner has broadened, among the more convincing cases have been fellow prisoners Charles de Batz d'Artagnan, Antonio Ercole Matthioli and Eustace Dauger. d'Artagnan was the famously indiscreet womanizer and captain of the First Company of Musketeers, who was imprisoned in the Bastille following a quarrel with Louis XIV's minister, Louvois. The theory goes he was in possession of embarrassing secrets about the king's close associates and whom Louvois had privately arranged to be imprisoned, without the king's knowledge.

Prison documentation has shown that the other candidates, Matthioli and Dauger, were the only two prisoners at Pignerol who could have been brought to the Bastille in 1698. Matthioli (to which the prisoner's burial name of Marchioly bears close resemblance) was an Italian diplomat who negotiated between the Duke of Mantua and the Republic of Venice in the selling of Casale. During negotiations, Matthioli double-crossed everyone involved and was eventually kidnapped by the French and thrown into Pignerol in 1679. However, because everyone knew about Matthioli's crimes there would have been no need to have kept his identity secret (and others claim that Matthioli died in 1681). The more likely candidate was the valet Eustace Dauger, whose master was the Huguenot Roux de Marsilly (Marchioly may be a misspelling of Marsilly?), and who had tried to stir up a Protestant alliance against France and was publicly tortured to death in Paris in 1669. Others have suggested that Dauger was a valet named 'Danger' or 'D'angers' who had botched a political assassination on behalf of the French secretary of state, however no theory has proved conclusive.

Despite the many colourful, convincing (and not so convincing) theories put forward, there is still no definitive answer to the Man in the Iron Mask's true identity, though it's safe to say the idea he was Louis XIV's brother – and indeed that the mask was made of iron – are without much foundation. The secrecy surrounding the unknown prisoner has bred a huge amount of speculation, embellishment and romantic fancy, to create a myth that now far outweighs the reality. It's a legend that has always gripped the public imagination, a story riddled with mystery that has in the process generated some of the very worst, but nonetheless entertaining, examples of 'bad history'.

Australia Was Established Purely as a Penal Colony, a Dumping Ground for Britain's Convicts

In 1788 a fleet of British ships arrived on the eastern shores of Australia. Alighting first at Botany Bay, where Lieutenant James Cook had landed eighteen years earlier, the fleet then moved on to the more suitable Port Jackson where they established a settlement at Sydney Cove on 26 January 1788. The fleet of eleven ships consisted of around 1,000 settlers, 751 of whom were British convicts sentenced to transportation to a land halfway across the world.

Over the next eighty years around 160,000 convicts were transported to the new Australian colonies of New South Wales, Van Diemen's Land (Tasmania) and Western Australia. The traditional view is that Australia was originally established by the British government purely as a kind of dumping ground for British convicts, as corroborated by historian Norman Bartlett in 1976: 'There is no evidence that either Prime Minister Pitt or any member of this cabinet thought of Botany Bay as anything more than a convenient place distant enough for the safe disposal of social waste.' It was a colonial experiment never tried before or since repeated.

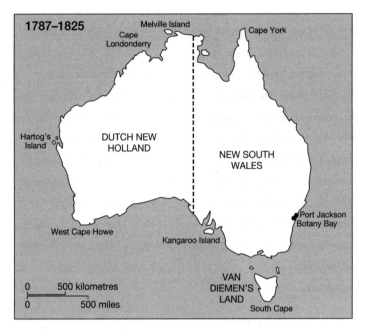

1787–1825

Melville Island

Cape York

Cape Londonderry

Hartog's Island

DUTCH NEW HOLLAND

NEW SOUTH WALES

Port Jackson Botany Bay

West Cape Howe

Kangaroo Island

VAN DIEMEN'S LAND

South Cape

| 0 | 500 kilometres |
| 0 | 500 miles |

A map of the colonization of Australia during the early stages of transportation

Yet others have challenged this assumption (including Geoffrey Blainey in *The Tyranny of Distance*) partly because there appears to be no logical sense in building a prison 12,000 miles away, unless there were deeper motives behind the decision. The unearthing of new sources has shed light on what these motives might have been. 'A Proposal for Establishing a Settlement in New South Wales' is one such document, and it was submitted to the government in 1783 by the American Loyalist James Matra, who had been aboard Cook's historic voyage to Botany Bay in 1770. Matra's justifications for settlement included: good soil suitable for sugar, cotton and tobacco plantation; the potential for whaling, flax cultivation and the availability of naval timber for the home market; and its usefulness as a trading base with China, Korea and Japan. Matra also proposed that the colony be settled by 'Americans who had remained loyal to Britain in the War of Independence' (such as himself), but this idea was ultimately rejected. It was only in 1784, following a meeting with Lord Sydney, Home Secretary, that the proposals were amended to include 'transportees [convicts] among the settlers as cultivators in their own right rather than as forced labour'. Now that convicts could no longer be sent to America (due to the War of Independence), the British government had been considering transporting convicts to West Africa (a much shorter and cheaper journey) but was ultimately swayed by Matra's more comprehensive proposal.

TRANSPORTATION

Transportation was an integral part of the English and Irish systems of punishment, and up until the American War of Independence around 1,000 criminals a year were sent to either Virginia or Maryland. British gaols and hulks (makeshift floating prisons) were full to bursting with rising numbers of criminals (due to an increased population) and transportation helped to relieve the pressure put on the British prisons.

A wide range of fairly minor offences could result in transportation and a number of the convicts sent in the early transports to Australia had only seven-year sentences. (Many of the women – who made up 20 per cent of the first convict settlers – were first-time offenders.) Had the government intended the colony of Australia to be nothing other than a gulag, one would have assumed they would have sent only the very worst convicts. Instead, a great majority of convicts were working men and women with a range of skills, whose seven-year sentences would provide enough time in which to set up the infrastructure of the colony. On later ships, convicts were also made up of political and social non-conformists such as Jacobin-types, Luddites and Ribbonmen, along with a smattering of wayward young men from the gentry and bourgeoisie classes (Charles Dickens sent two of his less academically gifted sons to Australia).

It is assumed that convicts bound for Australia suffered

appalling conditions (as deaths on board wouldn't have mattered to the authorities if they were simply seen as 'social waste'). Yet there is evidence to show that efforts were made to ensure the convicts arrived in relatively good health. Ships were inspected for sea-worthiness which Philip Knightley, in *Australia: Biography of a Nation* notes, made 'the convict voyage to Australia … distinctly safer than emigrant voyages either to Australia or to America.' Before transportation, many of the inmates were stripped of their vermin-infested clothes, bathed, and held for four days while being inspected by surgeons for infection, and many of the ships carried a surgeon-general whose main aim was to limit the number of deaths en route. Later ships, particularly those administered by private contractors, suffered higher death rates, although some of those deaths could have been borne from diseases previously contracted by prisoners. Whilst life on board the ships could indeed be brutal – prisoners were generally kept below deck in chains or behind bars – many of the convicts were provided with one substantial meal a day, religious instruction and even a daily dose of lemon juice to avoid scurvy.

Once the first convicts arrived at Botany Bay, they were not simply worked to death in a gulag-like prison but were integrated into a system of labour in which all people, whatever their crime, were employed. Convicts formed the majority of the colony's population in the first few decades, although the first free settlers (who were given free passage, land and provisions) also began arriving in 1793. Convicts were allocated work to suit their skills, and the unskilled were often involved in manual labour, such as road-building gangs. Conditions could be harsh and discipline was strictly enforced with flogging, leg irons or transportation to stricter penal colonies set up at Norfolk Island or Port Arthur. From 1801, some convicts were rewarded with Tickets of Leave that gave them certain freedoms, and by the 1820s few convicts served their full sentences. By the mid-1830s only around 6 per cent of the convict population were 'locked up', the majority working for free settlers and various other authorities. Transportation finally ended in 1868, when the population in Australia stood at a very healthy 1 million and the colonies were able to support themselves and grow without the need for convicts.

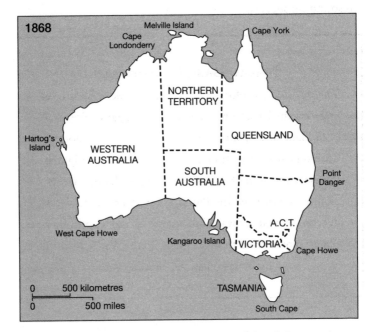

This map shows just how much Australia had changed towards the end of transportation

Although the transport of convicts to Australia did relieve the pressure put upon the prison authorities of Britain, the new colony was not viewed purely as a simple dumping ground for unwanted criminals. Australia's abundant resources, its strategic position and proximity to the Far East were also motivating factors, while the convicts provided a cheap labour force who could set up the infrastructure of the colony. Conditions for many of the transported convicts were brutal, but the establishment of Australia actually proved to be one of the more humane prison experiences of the eighteenth century and a social experiment (at least for the white settlers) that resulted in a resounding success.

Naval Base Potential

The decision to colonize New South Wales was also set against the backdrop of potential war against France, Holland and Spain. Matra showed how the colony would provide a useful naval base for attacks on Dutch possessions in the East Indies and Spanish colonies in South America and the Philippines. Over the next few decades, whenever war with Spain seemed a possibility, plans were revived to make New South Wales Britain's main naval base in the region.

President Roosevelt's New Deal Saved Capitalism and Lifted the US Out of the Depression

It's traditionally thought that President Hoover did nothing to tackle the Great Depression in America, whereas President Franklin D. Roosevelt confronted it head on, with a dazzling series of economic reforms known as the New Deal. This programme, passed by Congress between 1933 and 1936, rescued American capitalism and ultimately led to greater prosperity and renewed self-confidence. Roosevelt was hailed as the great saviour of capitalism and democracy, and a man who had restored belief and hope in America.

As Franklin D. Roosevelt took office in 1933, he promised a 'new deal' for the American people in the first one hundred days of his administration – a programme that would provide relief for the unemployed and poor, recover the nation's economy and reform the financial system. In a bid to stabilize the banking industry, Roosevelt closed all the banks until Congress passed the Emergency Banking Act (an act that had actually been carefully crafted by Treasury officials during Hoover's presidency). Sound banks could then open under Treasury supervision with federal loans if needed. In June 1933 the Federal Deposit Insurance Corporation (FDIC) was set up, which insured bank deposits of up to $2,500 and then $5,000. To deal with deflation, the

US currency was taken off the gold standard (except for foreign exchange) in the early spring of 1934. Other early reforms that formed part of Roosevelt's 'First New Deal' included: forcing businesses to set prices with the government and instituting regulations to prevent aggressive competition through the NRA (National Recovery Administration); setting minimum prices and wages; cutting agricultural production to raise prices through the Agricultural Adjustment Act. By 1935 the 'Second New Deal' added social security, a jobs programme for the unemployed and stimulus for the growth of trade unions through the National Labour Relations Board.

The economy temporarily improved and by 1937 industrial production exceeded levels of 1929, although unemployment remained at 11 per cent. In autumn 1937 the economy took another sharp downturn (largely as a result of the government reducing its support), and unemployment levels reached 19 per cent. The Depression lingered on, only lifting in 1941 when America joined the Second World War. Historian Doris Kearns Goodwin wrote: 'The America over which Roosevelt presided in 1940 was in its eleventh year of depression. No decline in American history has been so deep, so lasting, so far reaching.'

Roosevelt's New Deal programme of 'relief, recovery and reform' ultimately failed, and, according to some economists, actually caused the depression to persist longer than it otherwise would have done. The economists Harold L. Cole and Lee E. Ohanian in their 2004 article for the *Journal of Political Economy* maintained that Roosevelt's policies prolonged the downturn by as much as seven years and concluded that 'the New Deal policies

HOOVER'S FOUNDATIONS

Herbert Hoover's presidency (1929–33) coincided with the Wall Street Crash of 1929 and the ensuing Great Depression of the 1930s. Like his presidential forebears during earlier depressions, Hoover's first instinct was to do nothing, with the hope that the 'natural processes' of the economy would lead to an upturn. As the economy worsened, however, Hoover changed tactics and took firm action. At first he attempted to extract voluntary pledges from businesses to maintain production and employment levels, while encouraging state and municipal government to increase public works spending. When this failed, he turned to more direct federal intervention by increasing government spending on public works (the Hoover Dam and other construction projects cost the government some $50 million), buying up surplus farm produce through the Farm Board, and endorsing legislation to establish the Reconstruction Finance Corporation. The RFC, whose remit was to lend federal money to railroads, farmers and financial institutions, was to form a key agency of Roosevelt's New Deal. Although Hoover ultimately failed to reverse the depression (or provide relief for the poor), his presidential term initiated and provided the testing ground for a more direct federal interventionism.

[were] an important contributing factor to the persistence of the Great Depression.' Central to Cole and Ohanian's argument was the damaging effect of the NRA: its control of wages and prices effectively created industry-wide cartels that restricted production and raised prices, which distorted normal market conditions and prevented recovery. Roosevelt himself recognized this: 'The American economy has become a concealed cartel system [...] The disappearance of price competition is one of the primary causes of the present difficulties.'

Cole and Ohanian similarly argued that the Agricultural Adjustment Act worsened the situation by using tax revenue to pay farmers to restrict production. Not only did this put more pressure on the taxpayer, but it also led to a rise in food prices and substantial unemployment amongst farm workers (affecting as many as 2 million people). Although Roosevelt's first 100 days and intermittent radio broadcasts known as 'fireside chats' served to soothe the nation and boost public confidence, Roosevelt's critics claim that his administration led to a great deal of uncertainty and apprehension among American businessmen, discouraging much-needed long-term investment. Additionally, Roosevelt's massive funding of government-initiated projects certainly created jobs within the public sector, but economists John Joseph Wallis and Daniel K. Benjamin argue that revenues raised for these public ventures diverted capital and jobs from the private sector. These underlying and far less evident causes actually hampered the recovery of the private sector, added to long-term unemployment levels and had disastrous consequences for the economy.

On the surface, Roosevelt's reforms were impressive: he provided much-needed relief for the poor and those who could not help themselves; he constructed thousands of roads, schools and other public buildings; and he 'connected' with the American people with his brave series of interventionist measures. And yet many of the reforms of the New Deal served only to distort normal market conditions and prevent recovery of the private sector. Roosevelt was no saviour of capitalism; some of his reforms actually shackled the natural forces of the free market system and thereby hindered America's ability to pull itself out of depression.

Abraham Lincoln's Main Aim in Fighting the US Civil War Was to Free the Slaves

Abraham Lincoln is regarded as one of America's greatest presidents who successfully led his country through the Civil War of 1861–5, preserved the Union and abolished slavery throughout the US. It's commonly assumed that the issue of slave emancipation spurred Lincoln – a champion of racial equality – to invade the Southern states. An impressive theory, and worthy of such a fine president, but not quite true.

It took four years for the Union forces of the North to crush the Confederates of the South and in that time Lincoln's objectives in war changed. At the outset of hostilities, Lincoln had two basic aims: the preservation of the Union and to halt further expansion of slavery into the West. But as the war continued the abolition of slavery was to become his new and primary motive.

Although the slave-owning states of the South were convinced that Lincoln and his victorious Republican Party were hell-bent on emancipating their slaves, Lincoln at the outset of war was no abolitionist. At the end of his inaugural speech in March 1861 he stressed this specific point in an attempt to pacify the Southern secessionists: 'I have no purpose, directly or indirectly, to interfere with the institution of slavery in the States where it exists [...] We are not enemies but friends. We must not be enemies.' His words proved futile, however, as by 12 April Confederate

and Union troops were locked in battle at Fort Sumter, South
Carolina, and within weeks another four Southern states had joined
the Confederacy.

SOUTHERN SECESSION

When Lincoln became President in 1860, seven slave-
owning states in the South seceded from the Union
and formed the Confederate States of America (also
known as the Confederacy), electing Jefferson Davis
as their President. With the North growing in wealth
and population, the secessionists feared that Lincoln
and his victorious Republican Party would extend the
abolition of slavery across the US. Hostilities began in
1861 when Confederate troops fired on Union forces at
Fort Sumter in South Carolina (one of only two federal
properties in the South to remain in Union hands and
which Lincoln, although averse to war, refused to
surrender). Four more slave states joined the South's
fight for independence, and war was declared between
the Union forces (which included twenty mostly
northern free states and five border slave states)
and the Confederate army.

Prior to becoming President, Lincoln had frequently spoken
about his moral objections to slavery, although he often modified
his stance according to the audience he was addressing. To some,

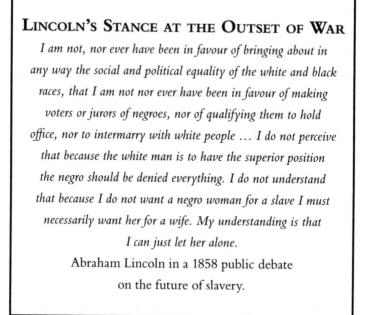

Lincoln's Stance at the Outset of War

I am not, nor ever have been in favour of bringing about in any way the social and political equality of the white and black races, that I am not nor ever have been in favour of making voters or jurors of negroes, nor of qualifying them to hold office, nor to intermarry with white people … I do not perceive that because the white man is to have the superior position the negro should be denied everything. I do not understand that because I do not want a negro woman for a slave I must necessarily want her for a wife. My understanding is that I can just let her alone.

Abraham Lincoln in a 1858 public debate
on the future of slavery.

he railed against the evil institution of slavery; to others he stressed the superiority of white over black (and in his home state of Illinois he never contested the inequality of blacks who could not vote or testify in court against whites). Lincoln's views on slavery came to the fore in 1858 when he engaged with Stephen A. Douglas, senior Senator for Illinois, in a series of highly publicized debates on the future of slavery in the United States. Douglas supported the view of 'popular sovereignty', that settlers in new territories should have the right to choose slavery. He tried to wreck Lincoln's chances of election by painting him as an out-and-out abolitionist. Lincoln adopted the Republican stance – slavery should be outlawed in the new territories to prevent its further spread. However, he made it clear that he had no intention to abolish slavery in the states where it already existed, nor was he a champion of racial equality. Still, at this stage Lincoln's key aim was to preserve the Union.

Preservation of the Union

In September 1862, Lincoln wrote a public letter to *Harper's Weekly* in which he said, 'If I could save the Union without freeing any slave I would do it, and if I could save the Union by freeing all the slaves I would do it. And if I could save it by freeing some and leaving others alone, I would also do that.'

Eight months into the Civil War Lincoln still looked to conciliate the Southern states and was adamant that the suppression of hostilities 'shall not degenerate into a violent and remorseless revolutionary struggle'. He even suggested to Congress that any slaves freed as result of the struggle be resettled abroad. Yet the war raged on and events soon slipped out of Lincoln's control. With so many Southern men fighting, the slave system they left behind began to disintegrate as slaves fled to Union lines. The untapped resources of escaped slaves proved more appealing to Lincoln and in July 1862 Congress passed legislation to allow the enlistment of black soldiers within the army. Reconciliation with the South no longer seemed possible, and more and more Northerners aligned themselves with the abolitionists. Still, Lincoln publicly maintained that his only goal was to save the Union, and that the pursuit of war was entirely divorced from the issue of slavery.

In September 1862 Lincoln announced an abrupt turnabout with the Emancipation Proclamation, which stated that all slaves of the Confederate States that did not return to Union control by 1 January 1863 would be freed – 3.1 million out of America's 4 million slaves would be liberated (the bill excluded roughly 800,000 slaves from the border states that were already part of the Union). Despite Lincoln's earlier intentions, the war had evolved into a revolutionary struggle for which slavery was now a key issue. Lincoln still maintained that his main purpose was preservation of the Union but recognized that this could now only be achieved through emancipation. In 1863, he wrote in a letter: 'The use of the colored troops constitute the heaviest blow yet dealt to the Rebellion, and that at least one of these important successes could not have been achieved when it was but for the aid of black soldiers.' By the time Lincoln delivered his famous Gettysburg address in November 1863, his public justification for war had shifted. Invoking the principles of the Declaration of Independence in which all men are created equal, he now defined the Civil War as a struggle not merely for the Union but as a new birth of freedom that would bring true equality to all of its citizens. After the passing of the Emancipation Proclamation, Lincoln lobbied Congress for a constitutional amendment outlawing slavery throughout America – this was finally passed on 31 January 1865.

Lincoln himself admitted that his standing on the issue of

emancipation changed through the course of the war. Although he was clearly opposed to slavery on ethical grounds, he did not seek its abolition at the outset of war, nor did he believe in racial equality. As the war progressed, however, conciliation with the South proved untenable, and emancipation became necessary for Lincoln's ultimate goal: the preservation of the Union. Lincoln summarized events in 1864, in a letter to Albert G. Hodges: 'I claim not to have controlled events, but confess plainly that events have controlled me. Now, at the end of three years' struggle the nation's condition is not what either party, or any man devised, or expected.'

THE GETTYSBURG MYTH

In November 1863, Lincoln was invited to speak at a funeral service for the lost soldiers of the Battle of Gettysburg fought four months earlier. Posterity tells us that he scribbled his famous three-minute speech of ten sentences (now one of the most quoted speeches in history) on the back of an envelope en route to the service. This is, in truth, a myth as Lincoln wrote the draft of his speech back in Washington and, according to David J. Eicher in *Gettysburg Battlefield*, took with him to the service five copies of the speech, none of which were written on the back of an envelope. The myth probably took hold because Lincoln's short and now legendary speech followed the two-hour (and now forgotten) speech of Massachusetts orator Edward Everett.

America Entered the First World War at the Last Minute and Contributed Little to the Allied Victory

It was (and still is) a commonly held belief, established during the latter years of the First World War, that America contributed little to the eventual victory of the Allies. Too proud to join in the conflict, America failed to offer practical help to those fighting on the Western Front and entered only so she could influence peace terms. But the reality is that America provided a crucial role in the Allied war effort both before and after she sent American troops to France.

At the outbreak of hostilities, President Woodrow Wilson stood firm by America's customary policy of isolation from the political affairs of Europe, a principle laid down by his country's Founding Fathers. America's melting-pot population of European peoples, of whom 8 million had been born in Germany, also added weight to the argument. Whilst his critics joked that Wilson was too timid to fight (shells that failed to explode were nicknamed by soldiers on the Western Front as 'Wilsons'), the President believed America had a unique moral role to play, which, he maintained, could stand above the war and shape its eventual peace.

Neutrality also gave a real boost to the economy of America, which in 1914 had been on the brink of recession. New markets

AMERICAN IMPORTS

Britain relied heavily on America for artillery, ammunition, aircraft and motor vehicles, and by 1916 30 per cent of British food was being imported from America. As the war progressed, US banks made massive loans to the Allied forces, lending, by the end of the war, 10 billion dollars to the Allies whilst the British blockaded much needed imports into Germany. These huge loans, imports of vital goods and the 'unwritten sympathy' by the US for the plight of Britain and her allies was of critical importance in the defeat of the Central Powers. As Gordon Corrigan in his book *Mud, Blood and Poppycock* maintains:

'American industry and American governmental tolerance were essential to the British war effort long before the United States entered the war, and while Britain might still have won the war without them, it would have taken far longer and would have taken many more lives.'

opened up around the world and increased demand from the warring nations boosted production and profit in the US. In practice, however, the Allies, and not the Central Powers, benefited mostly from America's increased industrial and agricultural output, thanks largely to its vast federal reserves and to Great Britain's tightly controlled naval blockade of Germany.

During the years 1914 to 1916 US exports to Great Britain and France multiplied from 750 million dollars to 2.75 billion dollars, whereas exports to Germany – which had fewer financial reserves than Britain and was concentrating on military expenditure – slumped from 345 million dollars to a mere 2 million dollars. The subsequent shortage in vital raw materials is considered by some to have been a major contributory factor to the eventual Allied victory.

It says here the War was
already won before we got here.

Early in 1917, the US was finally provoked to consider military action following the publication of the Zimmermann Telegram (which revealed the threat of a German/Mexican alliance) combined with all-out submarine warfare by German U-Boats against vessels of all kind, including neutral American ones. On 6 April 1917, the US declared war on Germany, although Wilson reasserted that the US had a different agenda to the Allies: 'We have no selfish ends to serve. We desire no conquest, nor dominion.' Wilson saw himself as having the moral upper hand, and he also clearly sought to influence, if not dictate, eventual peace terms. In July 1917 he maintained that 'England and France have not the same views with regard to the peace that we have by any means. When the war is over we can force them to our way of thinking, because by that time they will, among other things, be financially in our hands.'

Committed to war, the US rapidly set about preparing its fairly feeble military (ranked seventeenth in the world, alongside Argentina) for combat. Its army required enormous expansion, which the US achieved through the conscription of some 2.8 million men, while 24 million men were registered for the draft. The training of conscripts delayed matters, as did the acute shortage of ships to take them across the Atlantic, but by the end of 1917 around 200,000 American soldiers had been transported to Europe and by October 1918 around 1,800,000 US men were fighting on the Western Front.

The American Expeditionary Force took its first major action on 28 May 1918 when American soldiers – known as 'doughboys' – held the front line at Cantigny (with the help of French artillery) and eventually captured it from the Germans. In June, US forces drove the Germans out of Chateau Thierry and in July and August, nine US divisions helped with the Aisne-Marne counter-offensive, recapturing the Allied line between Reims and Soissons. At the end of September, over a million US soldiers (now formed into the First US Army) drove into the Argonne Forest towards the Hindenburg Line, but their inexperience and poor strategy brought heavy casualties, with 120,000 either dead or wounded. By the end of October, the British Third and Fourth Armies were over the River Selle, and all along the lines the Allied and American forces were advancing, whilst the Germans retreated. Morale among the German forces plummeted as defeat approached, and they were plagued with mutiny and desertion. The Allied forces, on the otherhand, attacked with, what Gordon Corrigan in *Mud, Blood and Poppycock* describes as, 'a seemingly inexhaustible supply of American manpower'.

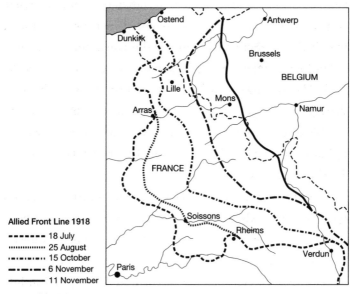

Allied Front Line 1918
- - - - - - 18 July
················· 25 August
·— ··— ··— ·· 15 October
—·—·—· 6 November
———— 11 November

A map of the Western Front, 1918

The massive autumn offensive, combined with the economic blockade of Germany, resulted in an abrupt end to hostilities, with the armistice coming into effect on 11 November 1918. Had the war continued beyond 1918, the American military could well have grown bigger than the combined forces of the British and French, and it was this knowledge that prompted General Ludendorff to launch the German offensive in the spring of 1918, a decision that cost him the war.

Whilst US casualties (over 100,000 deaths) were relatively low compared to those of the other Entente forces combined, they occurred in a short space of time and were keenly felt by the American nation, who had never before sent a mass army to a foreign war. The contribution of the Americans in the outcome of the First World War was critical: had they not supplied vital supplies, financial loans and, finally, their men, the war could have continued for several more gruelling years and may even have swung against an Allied victory.

THE GREAT FAMINE IN CHINA WAS THE UNINTENTIONAL CONSEQUENCE OF CHAIRMAN MAO'S ECONOMIC REFORMS

During the years 1958–61 the People's Republic of China underwent a series of economic and social reforms known as the Great Leap Forward. The Communist regime of Mao Zedong aimed to transform China into a modern Communist society with an economy and industrial output that would surpass that of the Soviet Union and Great Britain within fifteen years. Yet its programme of agricultural and industrial reforms, which included the prohibition of private farming and radical collectivization, led to catastrophe and the loss of millions of lives from starvation and deprivation. The idea that this loss of lives was an unintentional consequence of the Great Leap Forward disregards the Maoist regime's deliberate role in exacerbating the ensuing catastrophe.

Original estimates for 'excess deaths' during the Great Leap Forward ranged from 15 million to 32 million, yet the recent opening up of thousands of central and provincial documents, including secret party committee reports and public security documents, have revealed that these figures are woefully inadequate. This recent evidence suggests that at least 45 million people may have lost their lives prematurely during the years 1958–62. Frank Dikötter's book *Mao's Great Famine* draws from these new archival documents and describes how its victims were deliberately deprived of food and basic needs and worked to death or killed as a result of the systematic violence and terror. Dikötter argues that the word 'famine' fails to encompass the many ways people died, implying that the deaths were simply 'the unintended consequence' of the state's economic reforms. Instead, there was a large element of deliberate mass killing, and of systematic neglect of the type usually associated with Stalin, Hitler or Pol Pot, and one of the worst examples of mass murder in Chinese and world history.

Signs of famine first appeared in China in 1958; by the following year it was widespread. The new archive material shows that decisions made by the government's top officials led directly to severe food shortages and famine. Many of the regime's officials knew that people were starving to death, but those close to Mao indulged his visionary whims whilst others exaggerated the effectiveness of his reforms. Mao himself was aware of the famine and in 1959 he was quoted as saying, 'When there is not enough to eat people starve to death. It is better to let half of the people die so that the other half can eat their fill.'

Since 1953 farmers had been forced to sell grain to the state at prices determined by the government. However, during the years 1959–62, the new data shows that Mao's government increased the grain procurement quota from its usual 20–25 per cent to 30–37 per cent, at a time when the average output per head was at its lowest. Some of the grain the government procured was sold back to the farmers (at an inflated price) but much of it was exported or given as foreign aid to maintain China's reputation overseas. The needs of China's countryside were deliberately disregarded in favour of the government's 'export above all else' policy.

By the end of 1958, farms and households in China's countryside were collectivized into some 26,000 communes. Chinese society and its economy spiralled out of control as commune workers dismantled their houses to use as fertilizer, abandoned the fields to man makeshift steel furnaces (set up to achieve Mao's frenzied steel production targets) or to work on the government's mammoth and largely useless water conservation schemes, whilst their families died without food. Conditions were similarly appalling for many of China's industrial and factory workers, who were forced to meet ever increasing industrial output targets, and who also suffered from famine in large numbers (by 1961, up to half of the workforce in Beijing suffered from famine oedema).

Intimidation and coercion formed the foundation of Mao's regime, and anyone who questioned his policies was declared a 'rightist' and punished accordingly. Coercion of workers often escalated into extreme violence, from beatings by party officials to severe punishment and torture. It's now estimated that at least 6–8 per cent (around 2.5 million) of all the famine victims were killed or died of injuries inflicted by local officials or the militia. For the smallest offence, workers could also be sent to labour camps littered across China or to 're-education camps' or private gulags that were attached to most communes. Whilst much of the evidence is still undisclosed, it is estimated that there were around 8–9 million prisoners during each year of the Great Leap Forward, of which around 3 million people died in the labour camps during the famine. Suicide rates also grew exponentially, with between 1 and 3 million people killing themselves during the years 1958–62. Reports also show that people resorted to a variety of desperate measures to survive, from stealing and attacking granaries to abandoning their own children and even digging up the dead and eating them.

Mao's economic reforms led not just to a shortage of food but also to a shortage of all basic essentials. Approximately 30–40 per cent of China's housing was demolished, and millions of displaced peasants were left homeless, facing winters without firewood or adequate clothing (much of China's cotton was exported abroad or fed to the textile industries). The Great Leap Forward also had a disastrous impact on the natural resources of China, with the destruction of huge swathes of forest (50 per cent of all trees in some regions) whilst the government's irrigation schemes reduced crop fertility on farmlands and left whole regions devastated by heavy rain and typhoons.

Although Mao's famine has been known about in the West for many decades, few Westerners are aware of the scale or manner of the atrocities. As Professor Ilya Somin writes, 'Chinese Communist atrocities are little-known even by comparison to those inflicted by Communists in Eastern Europe and the Soviet Union, possibly because the Chinese are more culturally distant from Westerners than are Eastern Europeans.' The new archive material also confirms that the Chinese leadership was far from ignorant about the famine, and, as sinologist Roderick MacFarquhar writes, '[Mao] will be remembered as the ruler who initiated and presided over the worst manmade human catastrophe ever. His place in Chinese history is assured.'

THE LONG MARCH

The Long March represents a significant episode in the history of the Communist Party of China, marking the ascent to power of Mao Zedong as its leader. The official accounts tells us that between October 1934 and October 1935 the Central Red Army, under the guidance of Mao, fought its way north from Yudu in the Jiangzi province to Yan'an in the province of Shaanxi in a bid to escape from the Kuomintang (Chinese Nationalist Party). The over 80,000-strong army took 370 days to cover some 12,500 kilometres (8,000 miles) over very difficult terrain. The Long March came to seal the personal prestige of Mao, who oversaw the defeat of the Nationalist forces and its leader Chiang Kai-shek. The legend surrounding the Long March, however, does not quite tally with the actual events. To begin with, there was not one Long March but a series of marches by various Communist armies. Mao did not control or even plan the march and was only told about it a couple of days beforehand. By the time the Red Army reached Yan'an, Mao was in full control but he did not single-handedly defeat Chiang Kai-shek. Instead Kai-shek's own commanders had defected, kidnapped Kai-shek and forced him to recognize the Communists so that they could all fight their common enemy: the Japanese.

THE SUFFRAGETTES SECURED
VOTES FOR WOMEN IN BRITAIN

In the early part of the twentieth century, British suffragettes, under the leadership of Emmeline Pankhurst, waged a bitter and much publicized campaign to secure the vote for women. Under the rally cry of 'Deeds not Words', they used daring and sometimes violent methods, from organizing mass marches and smashing windows to arson attacks on public buildings and refusing food when imprisoned. When women were finally given the vote by the government in 1918, it was widely attributed to the militant actions of the suffragettes. However, although the suffragettes generated considerable publicity and added to the pressure put on government, their campaign was only one part of a wider movement that led eventually to the enfranchisement of women.

Since the 1850s, women in Victorian Britain had campaigned for better rights and by the 1870s women's suffrage societies had been set up all over the country. In 1897, Millicent Garrett Fawcett grouped these societies to form the National Union of Women's Suffrage Societies, whose members were called the suffragists. They campaigned for women to have the vote on the same terms as men and aimed to convert public opinion through peaceful methods. Working within existing political channels, the suffragists held meetings, issued leaflets and supported male candidates who were in favour of votes for women. Their numbers grew rapidly and in 1907, 3,000 women marched under the banner of the NUWSS –

an astonishing sight for people who had never before seen women marching in public. The suffragists continued to win support for the cause of women's suffrage right up to the start of the First World War, by which time they had more than 50,000 members.

The more left-leaning Women's Social and Political Union (later known as the suffragettes) was set up by Emmeline Pankhurst in 1903, with the aim of securing the vote for women, as well as improving their social conditions. They at first worked with the NUWSS, and in 1908 they jointly held a large and well-attended march in London. When Prime Minister Asquith still withheld the vote from women, the WSPU turned to more confrontational tactics. Over the next two years, suffragettes tried to break in and smash government office buildings, and when they were imprisoned many of them went on hunger strike and were later force-fed by the authorities. In 1910 the government invited both the NUWSS and the WSPU to draw up the Conciliation Bill to give votes to women. By the end of 1911 the bill had yet to be passed, so the suffragettes stepped up their militancy. They smashed windows and damaged public buildings, set fire to letterboxes and destroyed thousands of letters, and on occasion they set off bombs (Emmeline Pankhurst, who emphasized her full responsibility for all acts of militancy among her followers, received a three-year sentence after Lloyd George's house suffered bomb damage. She served only six weeks of the sentence because the WSPU halted its militancy in August 1914). And in 1913 Emily Davison famously threw herself in front of the king's horse at the Derby and was killed (see p.104).

THE ULTIMATE SACRIFICE

On 4 June 1913 Emily Davison, a highly educated and committed suffragette, slipped past the barriers at the famous Epsom Derby, and threw herself in front of the oncoming horses. She was knocked down by King George V's horse, Anmer, trampled by those that followed, and died in hospital four days later. The suffragette movement quickly asserted that she had deliberately given her life for the 'Votes for Women' cause. The inquest into her death, however, concluded that she didn't set out to commit suicide but simply wished to interrupt the race. Eyewitnesses were divided on what caused her actions: some suggested that she only wanted to attach the suffragette banner to the king's horse whilst others saw her grab at the reins. On (admittedly very grainy) footage it looks as if she didn't throw herself down before the horses but was standing up before she was struck. People who knew her reported that she wasn't suicidal, she hadn't written a suicide note, and had even bought a return train ticket to the derby. Although her protest was undoubtedly bold and dangerous, it's unlikely suicide was her goal.

Although the increased publicity led to a boost in suffragette membership, Millicent Fawcett was convinced that the suffragettes' violent methods were damaging the cause and from 1908 onwards dissociated the NUWSS from the suffragette movement. Newspapers increasingly ran unfavourable reports on the suffragette protests, depicting activists as irrational, even deranged creatures (the term 'suffragette' was originally a disparaging label bandied by the *Daily Mail*), convincing some people that women could not be trusted with the vote. Similarly, the extremist behaviour of the suffragettes alienated MPs who had previously been sympathetic to women's suffrage.

By the time the First World War broke out, both the WSPU and the NUWSS had halted their political activities and instead campaigned for women to help with the war effort. By the end of the war women were involved in a wide range of jobs traditionally seen as the preserve of men, including factory work, coal mining, office work and farming. At the same time, Lloyd George, who was more sympathetic toward female suffrage, had replaced Asquith as Prime Minister in 1916. In the following year, the House of Commons extended the suffrage, initially to ensure that returning soldiers who hadn't been resident in Britain could vote, and then to include munition workers – which inevitably led the government to consider female munition workers who made up a large part of their number. In 1918, the Representation of the People Act was given royal assent, which gave the vote to women aged thirty and over, as well as to men aged twenty-one and over, and also allowed women to stand for election.

Although the suffragettes had generated awareness for the cause of women's rights, it was the First World War and its impact on democracy that finally gave the impetus for reform. The extraordinary circumstances of the war, in which the jobs of many of the men who were conscripted were taken by women, helped to change people's attitudes about women's role in society. The suffragettes' extreme methods certainly aroused a passionate and much needed debate about women's inequality, but their actions sometimes generated questions about their ability to work within a peaceful political establishment. The suffragists and the Victorian feminists before them, together with the female workers of the Great War, also played a crucial part in finally securing the vote for women in Britain.

James Watt Invented the Steam Engine

The Scottish-born mechanical engineer James Watt invented the steam engine and thus created the driving force behind the Industrial Revolution. Well, yes and no. The man revered as one of the founding fathers of the Industrial Revolution (so much so that his name was used for the SI power unit, the 'watt') *did* invent a type of steam engine that could be used in factories or mills, but he *didn't* invent the *first* steam engine.

Indeed, prior to Watt, quite a lot of work had already been done on the principle of the steam engine (which is, in essence, using boiling water to produce mechanical motion). Watt himself adapted a machine that had already been invented by Thomas Newcomen some seventy years earlier. Newcomen's atmospheric steam engine, first introduced in 1712, employed a piston and cylinder and was used to pump water from deep coal mines in Britain and in Europe.

THE HISTORY BEHIND THE ENGINE

The history of the steam engine is rich and varied. Before Newcomen, Thomas Savery had by 1698 patented and constructed a similar water pump engine, the 'Miner's Friend'. Newcomen himself had based his engine on the experiments of Frenchman Denis Papin who in 1679 invented a 'steam digester', a device that extracted fats from bones in a high-pressured steam environment (the forerunner of the domestic pressure cooker). Even the Ancient Greeks had a stab at making a steam engine, with a contraption called the 'aeolipile', which consisted of a hollow globe that spun on its axis when steam pressure was applied through pipes.

Watt's genius lay in the improvements he made to Newcomen's engine, so that it could be used in all sorts of industrial settings and not just for pumping water out of coal mines. Between 1763 and 1764 Watt, whilst working at Glasgow University, was asked to repair a model Newcomen engine. Noting that the engine design wasted energy by repeatedly heating and cooling the cylinder, Watt proposed that it use two cylinders, one that remained hot and one, called the condensor, that remained cold and was separated from the piston chamber. This alteration radically boosted the engine's power, improved its efficiency and saved on coal costs. Working closely with the manufacturer Matthew Boulton, Watt made further alterations to the steam engine, and by 1783 he had developed a double-acting rotative type of engine, adding a flywheel and 'governor' so that the speed of the engine could be made constant. This new type of engine could be used to drive the machinery of factories and mills, and by 1800 the firm Boulton & Watt had constructed some 449 engines for use in industry.

Diagram of the Greek engine, the aeolipile

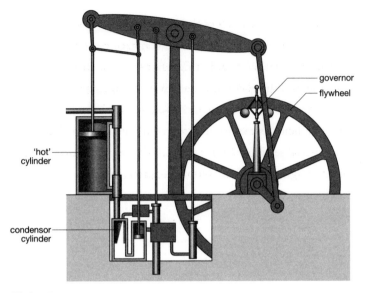

Watt's engine

However, contrary to popular belief, the steam engine was not immediately taken up by industry in the nineteenth century; its introduction was gradual and many manufacturers in the first half of the century continued to rely on traditional forms of power, namely water, horse and human power. The newer industries, however, in particular the cotton trade, made great use of the steam engine and mines, waterworks, canals and ironworks were particularly reliant on steam power. Later adaptations were made to Watt's engine so that steam power could also be used in locomotives, furnaces and steam boats. Its use also led to the development of the machine tool industry, which allowed machines to be constructed in ever greater complexity. The real surge in the application of steam power occurred in the latter half of the nineteenth century, particularly when it was used to drive turbines generating electricity.

Whilst James Watt didn't develop the first steam engine – that responsibility lay with the primitive contraption invented by the Ancient Greeks – he did play a vital role in developing a type of efficient steam engine that could be used in all manner of industrial settings. And it was this development that allowed for the engine's gradual adoption across industry during the nineteenth century.

CECIL RHODES: HEROIC BRITISH IMPERIALIST OR EVIL ROGUE?

The memory of Cecil Rhodes (1853–1902) deeply divides those who consider his legacy. In the twentieth century, when it was fashionable in Britain to celebrate the achievements of the Empire builders, Rhodes was revered as a great hero of imperial history, a man who colonized vast tracts of southern Africa, conceived the ambitious Cape to Cairo Railway and gave his name to Rhodesia. These days he's viewed less favourably: as a crook, an arrogant bully and a ruthless diamond magnate who schemed his way to political prominence, whilst championing the cause of white supremacy. Opinion is polarized between national hero and national embarrassment, but is this an over-simplified approach?

Many historians agree that Rhodes was a flawed character, but he was also a complex man – ruthless and bigoted as well as shrewd and immensely ambitious. And yet we also know very little about his personal intimacies as he left no revealing letters to his loved ones. His friend Rudyard Kipling warned that 'Rhodes's personality would be a very difficult thing to translate to a man who did not know him well,' whilst the historians Robert I. Rotberg and Miles F. Shore in *The Founder: Cecil Rhodes and the Pursuit of Power* wrote, 'He was larger than life and the favour and enmity that his name still evokes are appropriate responses.'

Rhodes, a sickly, asthmatic teenager, was first sent from England to the improving climate of South Africa in 1870. A year later he moved to Kimberley and for the next two years he and his brother joined the rush to exploit South Africa's diamond and gold deposits. In 1873, having made a tidy sum of £10,000, he returned to England as an undergraduate at Oriel College, Oxford, at a time when the rousing words of John Ruskin filtered through the corridors. Ruskin urged the youth of England 'to found colonies as fast as she is able [...] seizing upon any piece of fruitful waste ground she can set her foot on and there teaching her colonists that their chief virtue is fidelity to their country'.

On returning to South Africa, Rhodes proved himself an astute businessman and by 1880 he had established control of the diamond mines and formed the De Beers Mining Company. By 1890 De Beers had become the largest company in southern Africa, Rhodes controlled 90 per cent of the world's diamond market and he had risen to become Prime Minister of Cape Colony.

CAPE TO CAIRO RAILWAY

Cecil Rhodes envisioned a continual 'red line' of British dominions between the north and south of Africa. As part of this plan, he initiated the Cape to Cairo railway at the end of the nineteenth century. The line was never fully completed, although large parts of it are still operating either side of Uganda and the northern Sudan.

Rhodes also headed up the British South Africa Company, through which he hoped to colonize much of south-central Africa. In 1889, Rhodes obtained a Royal Charter to develop the region north of the Transvaal and, through the Rudd Concession, King Lobengula of Matabeleland granted him exclusive mining rights in the Ndebele territory, in exchange for money and weaponry. However, the illiterate king had been duped into signing a document that failed to contain the promises he had verbally agreed with Rhodes's agents. Once Lobengula became aware of the scale of Rhodes's mining operation he tried, unsuccessfully, to renounce the concession. In 1893, Lobengula was eventually forced into a war he had no hope of winning, and Rhodes's troops seized his kingdom, which became part of Southern Rhodesia (now Zimbabwe) and they also seized control of Northern Rhodesia (now Zambia).

The cheating and the subjugation of the Ndebele is indeed a sorry story, although Lobengula himself had gained some notoriety as a tyrant, having wiped out many of the Mashona people when he colonized their land only a generation before. Others, too, had their eye on the lands north of South Africa, to include the Transvaal Boers, not to mention the Germans, Belgians and Portuguese, who could similarly have moved into the Ndebele or Mashona territories had Rhodes not got there before them. As the Rhodesian-born journalist Peter Godwin has written, 'Rhodes and his cronies fit[ted] in perfectly with their surroundings and conformed to the morality (or lack of it) of the day.'

Famous Quotes of Rhodes

'Remember that you are an Englishman, and have consequently won first prize in the lottery of life.'

When asked by Jameson how long he would endure in memory, Rhodes replied, 'I give myself four thousand years.'

'I would annex the planets, if I could; I often think of that.'

By our modern standards, Rhodes behaved appallingly towards the people of southern Africa, much of it bolstered by his unflinching belief in imperialism. 'I contend that we [the British] are the first race in the world,' he wrote, 'and the more of the world we inhabit the better it is for the human race.' He was a fierce proponent of the virtues of the Anglo-Saxon race, although his close colleagues, in particular his great friend Dr Jameson, wrote of Rhodes's great 'affinity' with the African people, 'he is really, by nature, strangely and deeply in sympathy with the natives … He regards them as children, with pity in his affection for them, and he treats them like children, affectionately but firmly.'

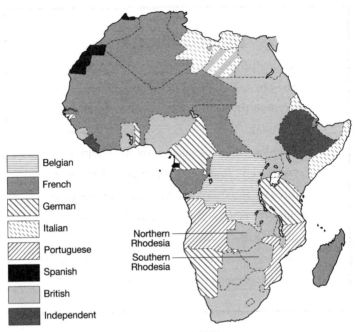

Belgian

French

German

Italian

Portuguese

Spanish

British

Independent

Northern Rhodesia

Southern Rhodesia

A map of colonial Africa on the eve of the First World War

Rhodes was, in essence, a man of his time, who was a racist like many of his contemporaries, and unscrupulous in many of his endeavours. Yet he also had enormous drive and vision and it could be argued that he behaved no worse than the white settlers in Australia or North America, where the indigenous people were very nearly wiped out. He was also a curious mix of the good and bad – and his achievements, even at the time of his death, attracted both praise and contempt. His obituary in *The Times* read: 'He has done more than any single contemporary to place before the imagination of his countrymen a clear conception of the Imperial destinies of our race [but] we wish we could forget the other matters associated with his name.'

THE JAMESON RAID

Rhodes suffered a severe blow to his reputation when in 1895 Dr Leander Starr Jameson led a force into the Transvaal in an illegal attempt to overthrow the Boer government. Secretly supported by Rhodes, who had a design on the wealth of the Transvaal, the campaign was a disaster. Jameson was captured by Boer forces, Rhodes was disgraced and relations between the Boers and the British worsened, leading to the South African War of 1899–1902. Rhodes was forced to resign from the Cape Colony, never returned to office and died in 1902.

THE ATTACK ON PEARL HARBOR WAS DELIBERATELY ENGINEERED BY PRESIDENT ROOSEVELT

On the morning of 7 December 1941, the Japanese launched a ferocious and sudden airborne attack on the US Pacific Fleet stationed at Pearl Harbor, on the Hawaiian island of Oahu. The Japanese succeeded in sinking or badly damaging eight US battleships, three destroyers, three cruisers and killing or wounding 3,435 servicemen. The 'date which will live in infamy', as President Franklin D. Roosevelt called it, not only sparked the Pacific War but also ensured that America would be drawn into war in Europe.

With a large part of the US naval strength at anchor during the attack, American forces had clearly been ill-prepared for the assault, and rumours almost immediately circulated as to how and why the United States had been caught off its guard. Some theorists (in books such as *The Skeleton in Uncle Sam's Closet* by Hartford Van Dyke, published in 1973) have argued that Roosevelt provoked the Japanese into attacking in a bid to maintain his own political security whilst also giving him just cause to enter the Second World War. The argument rages on and even today, conspiracy theorists argue that American officials, from the President down, had prior knowledge of Japan's intentions but were persuaded to keep silent.

Although the attack was swift and sudden, relations between

the US and Japan had been worsening for years – and it was this that ultimately pushed Japan into war with the US. Since the early 1930s the US had become increasingly alarmed by Japan's mounting aggression against China. War in Europe led to Japan signing the Tripartite Axis Pact with Germany and Italy in September 1940, with Japan now focusing its attention on British, French and Dutch colonies in South-East Asia. In response to Japanese aggression, the US continued to impose heavy embargoes on Japan, and by July 1941 trade between the two countries ceased entirely. Three months later, the moderate government in Tokyo was taken over by the more militant General Tojo ('the Razor') who took a more hard-line approach in his negotiations with the US. American officials responded in a similar vein, announcing that the US would only resume trade with Japan if Japanese troops were withdrawn from China and Indochina and Japan supported the Nationalist government in China. With neither country backing down, negotiations ended in deadlock.

In fact, the US administration knew that Japan had set a deadline for a diplomatic solution, after which, if an agreement hadn't been achieved, they would go to war. US cryptanalysts had cracked Japanese diplomatic codes and US decoding machines named 'Magic' enabled the Americans to read confidential Japanese messages. However, the problem with the 'Magic' messages were that thousands had to be deciphered, translated and evaluated, and they never revealed when or where an attack would be made. The Roosevelt administration knew that an assault was imminent but they assumed the Japanese would strike somewhere in South-East Asia. It never occurred to them that the Japanese would target the heavily fortified island of Oahu.

Americans also seriously underestimated the military capabilities of Japan, and wrongly assumed that Japan was unable to mount more than one naval operation at a time. US officials were totally unaware that a Japanese carrier task force comprising six aircraft carriers (having embarked on 26 November) was crossing the western Pacific towards Pearl Harbor as the Japanese skilfully maintained complete radio silence and avoided sea lanes used by merchant ships.

On 6 December 'Magic' began decoding a fourteen-part message from Tokyo to the Japanese delegation in Washington. The final part of the message apparently instructed the Japanese delegation to break off negotiations, thus hinting at war. However, there was a delay getting the translated version of the message to the Secretary of State and Chief of the US General Staff so that by the time officials received it at Pearl Harbor, the attack had already begun. For decades it was thought that this was why the US had had no prior warning of the attack; however, academics have recently argued that this last document didn't amount to anything as clear-cut as a declaration of war, or a breaking-up of diplomatic relations, as the Japanese had no intention of formally declaring war or even giving prior notice to any ending of negotiation.

Aside from America's inability to decipher Japan's exact motives, Roosevelt himself was in no hurry for war. He knew that America needed more time to build up its military capacity and, if anything, wanted to postpone hostilities with Japan for as long as possible as he saw the war against the Nazis in Germany as more of a priority. And even when war with Japan became increasingly likely, there is evidence to show that Roosevelt wanted to avoid appearing as the aggressor. On 6 December, in answer to an adviser's question as to why the US didn't strike first to 'prevent any sort of surprise', he responded, 'No, we can't do that. We are a democracy and a peaceful people.'

HIT AND RUN

The Pearl Harbor attack was designed to be a surprise hit-and-run raid. The Japanese planned to immobilize the US fleet while they conquered crucial targets in South-East Asia – to include the Philippines, Burma and Malaya – which were rich in assets like tin, rubber and oil. Japan lacked natural resources and, following trade embargoes by the US, she desperately needed to secure alternative supplies. Japan also hoped that destroying the US Pacific Fleet would crush American morale and cause Roosevelt to sue for peace (although it ultimately had the opposite effect in uniting the country behind war against Japan).

Since the attack, the US government has made nine official inquiries (from 1941 to 1995), all of which have shown there is no foundation to the argument that Roosevelt knew about the impending attack on Pearl Harbor and deliberately failed to prevent it. Rather, the inquiries have pointed to a general underestimation of Japanese capabilities as well as impaired coordination between the army and navy (i.e. Washington and Oahu) and lack of manpower in the processing of intelligence – all of which suggests incompetence and human error rather than deliberate conspiracy. Indeed, Roosevelt was privy to the same information as his officials: they were warned of imminent Japanese action but their biggest mistake was to underestimate the military capabilities of Japan and assume that a strike on Pearl Harbor was inconceivable.

The Yamamoto Myth

The Japanese Admiral Isoroku Yamamoto, who conceived the attack, is famously said to have told his officers, 'I fear all we have done is to awaken a sleeping giant and fill him with a terrible resolve.' A memorable line – which in film adaptations makes for a dramatic scene – but, sadly, there is no record that Yamamoto actually said it.

The 'Madness' of King George III Was Caused by the Blood Disease Porphyria

In the later part of his life, George III (1738–1820) suffered recurrent periods of mental disturbance and delirium, which his physicians were unable to control. He first showed signs of serious mental illness in 1788 and finally succumbed to permanent mania and dementia in 1810. In the mid-1960s mother and son psychiatrist team Ida Macalpine and Richard Hunter attributed the King's condition to the inherited blood disorder porphyria, a rare disease that can lead to epileptic-like seizures and mental illness. Yet, according to psychiatrist Timothy Peters of the University of Birmingham, this diagnosis has never been substantiated and recent research has shown that much of it was based on selective interpretation of evidence. In 2010, Peters and historian Dr David Wilkinson re-examined the huge amount of available data and concluded that bipolar disorder (also called manic depression) was a far more probable explanation for the King's condition.

Key to the diagnosis of porphyria were the King's six episodes of 'discoloured urine' (which Peters argues is not in itself a feature of acute porphyria). A detailed examination of the records show that the blue urine followed six reports of normal yellow urine during the same six weeks. Three days before the blue urine, the King was given a prescription of extract of gentian to stimulate digestion and this may well have caused the discoloration. Records from 1788 detail the King's increasingly disturbed behaviour ranging from incessant talking and rambling to physical violence and sexual indiscretions and even 'the most beastly indecency' of priapism (persistent penile erection). Whereas acute porphyria is more commonly associated with impotence, priapism is an occasional feature of acute mania and manic-depressive psychosis.

THE EVIDENCE

There is a vast amount of evidence relating to the King's mental health, not least the 100 volumes of medical notes written by George's numerous physicians (including those of the Willis family of 'mad doctors', Dr Francis Willis and his sons John and Robert Darling Willis). Copious letters, diaries and comments by politicians and aides also give valuable first-hand information on the King's illnesses. Few historians have trawled through all of the available data, although, according to Dr Peters, 'a morning in the British Library examining the relevant papers about Francis Willis, who with his sons, treated the King for madness, is time enough to expose the "blue urine myth"'.

More recent psychiatric assessments of the evidence relating to the King's condition fit the modern criteria for bipolar disorder.

The King's four episodes of acute mania, all of which lasted between three and five months, were characteristic of patients suffering from manic depression. George's final episode between 1810 and 1820, during which he progressed to chronic mania and dementia, was also indicative of untreated bipolar disorder. The King's illnesses also seemed to occur alongside periods of stress and significant historic events. George himself blamed his final bout of illness in 1810 to the stress surrounding the death of his youngest and favourite daughter Princess Amelia.

MACALPINE AND HUNTER'S THESIS

Macalpine and Hunter believed that mental illnesses were primarily caused by physical diseases and their diagnosis of George III – whose malady, they wrote, 'was not "mental" in the accepted sense' – formed part of their overall thesis designed to challenge contemporary attitudes to mental illness. In a summary to their first paper, they wrote, 'this diagnosis clears the House of Hanover of an hereditary taint of madness', an approach that seemed to reinforce negative attitudes to mental illness, and which was subsequently criticized by fellow medics. In 1998, Roy Porter wrote in *The Lancet*, 'Macalpine made much of the notion that the King had at last been rescued from what she called the taint of madness – he had, thank goodness, been suffering all the time from a nice clean, respectable organic disease.'

The King also suffered a range of physical illnesses, from fever to abdominal and chest pain, much of which Macalpine and Hunter linked to porphyria. However, physical ailments are common to those who suffer from bipolar disorder – in a 1990 study of 302 hospitalized manic patients, 70 per cent had digestive and abdominal symptoms (as George III did). Infections such as influenza are also known to lead to manic behaviour and at the onset of each of the King's episodes the records tell us that he suffered from a head cold or 'bilious fever'. George may also have suffered from obsessive-compulsive disorder (he dated his letters to the minute), which is another feature of bipolar disorder and which may explain his obstinate inflexibility over the US colonies.

In addition, had George III inherited porphyria, then half of his fifteen children and eight siblings would have also inherited the porphyric gene, and at least a couple would normally have shown symptoms. (As far as we know this wasn't the case.) Although many medical historians have claimed that some of George's ancestors and descendants suffered from porphyria, to include Mary Queen of Scots and even Princess Margaret, this has never been proven.

Thus, it is unlikely that George III suffered from porphyria. A reassessment of all the available data shows that Macalpine and Hunter's diagnosis was flawed and symptomatic of contemporary attitudes to mental health. The evidence now points to a manic-depressive disorder – a disease less stigmatized today but no less tragic for the King. The 'blue urine myth' looks to have finally been debunked.

Britain Was Once a Fully Integrated Province of the Roman Empire

The invasion of Britain by Roman legions in AD 43 ushered in the golden age of 'Roman Britain'. Under the aegis of the imperial city of Rome, Britain was to become a land of towns and villas, baths and gymnasiums as toga-clad Britons went about their daily Roman lives. It's an appealing image and one that contrasts starkly with the seemingly primitive era of pre-Roman Iron Age Britain.

At least they made the wagons run on time!

Yet during 400 years of Roman occupation, Britain was never fully integrated into the Roman Empire, nor did its inhabitants necessarily think of themselves as Romans. As shown by Miles Russell and Stuart Laycock in *UnRoman Britain*, the Roman conquest of Britain was viewed by many as a 'strategic failure': its legions failed to conquer the northern parts of the country (and never even attempted to invade Ireland) and Britain remained a frontier land, the 'Wild West' of the Roman Empire.

ROMAN ROADS

Recent archaeological excavations suggest that pre-Roman British tribal kingdoms planned and built roads that were just as good as Roman ones. Findings in Shropshire have found examples of an Iron Age road, which was properly engineered and surfaced with layers of brushwood, silt and cobbles. Archaeologists believe the Iron Age road may have been up to forty miles long, connecting an important Iron Age hilltop settlement near Telford with another key 'Old Oswestry' hilltop in Shropshire. The highway continued to be used into the Roman period, and suggests that some Roman roads were built directly on top of prehistoric ones constructed by early Britons.

Nonetheless, the Roman occupation of Britain evolved, particularly in the nineteenth century, into a much cherished period of British history. The wealth of archaeological remains in Britain testify to the enduring legacy of Rome, whereas little survives to inform us about life in pre-Roman Britain. Iron-age hilltop forts, or *oppida,* are dotted around the country, but no permanent structures from the period have remained (as early Britons built in wood and mud). The only contemporary written descriptions come from Greek and Roman authors, who predictably depicted early Britons as primitive and backward. In the late first century BC, the Greek historian Diodorus Siculus tells us that the Britons were 'simple in their habits and far removed from the cunning and vice of modern man'. And yet society in late Iron Age Britain was probably less primitive in outlook than we think: tribal territories were expanding, settlements were becoming more centralized and from around the second century BC there is evidence of trade between Europe and Britain.

Unlike her European neighbours, Britain was never fully integrated into the Roman Empire, partly because her tribal network fought hard to maintain its independence (and would remain intact after the Romans' arrival). During the thirty years after invasion, the Roman army gradually conquered most of southern England but only through a combination of treaties with tribal leaders (who were allowed to keep their land in return for their loyalty) and decisive military action. Throughout the first century AD, the Romans faced a series of tribal revolts, including the Iceni revolt in AD 60, which under the leadership of Boudicca destroyed the Roman towns of Colchester, London and St Albans and almost spelt the end of Roman rule. The crushing of the Boudiccan revolt was followed by a period of expansion and between AD 77 and 83 the new governor, Agricola, took in all of Wales, northern England and southern Scotland. During the next century tribal risings in Scotland and commitments in other parts of the Roman Empire forced Roman troops to retreat south to the frontier of Hadrian's Wall in northern England, where they remained for the next 250 years.

Rome's failure to conquer Scotland and the long-term stationing of a significant proportion of the entire Empire army in the north hindered the integration of the tribal elite, and the north remained a problematic area for the Romans. In many areas of Britain, particularly the northern and western extremities of England, as well as some parts of Wales (where the indigenous Celtic language survives as Welsh), tribal communities continued to live in Iron Age-style round houses on small settlements, much as they had before the invasion.

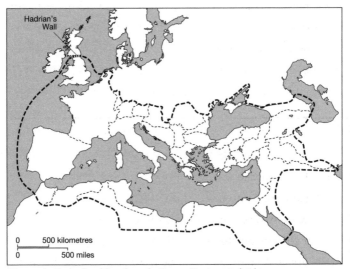

The area inside the dotted line shows the Roman Empire at its height

Whilst the Romans managed to establish effective control in southern, central and eastern parts of England, even here, as Russell and Laycock argue, their occupation had little impact on those who lived outside the newly built towns, villas and military forts. In keeping with the classical ideal of urban life, the Romans built a network of towns in Britain divided into regions called *civitates*. These towns, complete with markets, basilicas, baths and theatres, were to replace the early Iron Age hilltop forts. And yet compared to other provinces of the Roman world, Roman Britain had few towns and, as Laycock and Russell suggest, these towns demonstrated a 'broad continuity' with the later Iron Age as they still functioned as tribal centres, run by the native elite, albeit surrounded by new buildings and markets. Although the towns' native elites were courted by the Roman authorities, and the rich and the powerful did latch on to Roman art and culture – Tacitus wrote that his father-in-law, Agricola, 'gave private encouragement and public aid to the building of temples … [and] provided a liberal education for the sons of the chiefs – the vast majority of people living in the towns were largely unaffected by it.

REBEL ARMY

By the end of the second century AD, more Britons were being absorbed into the Roman army, and throughout the following two centuries the legions became notorious for their chronic rebelliousness. Resentment grew amongst the natives as taxes soared in the third century, and by the end of the fourth, Britons had had enough, and walked out of the Empire. The traditional view is that rampaging Saxons put an end to Roman culture, but significant Saxon settlement occurred long after the main collapse of Roman culture.

Outside of the towns, Roman villas exhibited some of the finest examples of Roman art. Yet despite the large number of sites excavated across Britain, Romanized villas represented less than 2 per cent of the known rural settlement pattern during the Roman occupation. In the agricultural areas of England and Wales, the nature of food production and settlement type appears to have changed little from the early Iron Age into the Roman period, and farms from the Roman period often occupy the same plot as their Iron Age predecessors. Rural people (who still made up the great majority of the population) may have bought the odd Roman object or picked up minor aspects of Roman culture, but their general settlement patterns and the basic rhythms of life were largely unaffected by Roman occupation.

Once the Romans withdrew from Britain, the influence of Roman culture pretty much ground to a halt, far more completely than in any other Roman province, many of which continued to speak their own version of Latin (whereas the English took up the West Germanic language of their Anglo-Saxon invaders). Throughout the occupation by Rome, the majority of Britons retained their tribal affiliations, and Britannia remained a troublesome and unenthusiastic member of the Roman Empire, which never fully embraced the far-flung ideals of Ancient Rome.

THE ITALIAN ASTRONOMER GALILEO WAS PERSECUTED BY THE CATHOLIC CHURCH, AND IMPRISONED IN A DARK CELL

The myth holds that in the seventeenth century the Roman Catholic Church convicted the elderly scientist Galilei Galileo (1564–1642) for heresy, whereupon he was tortured and left to rot in a dark cell. The 'Galileo Affair' was perceived as a battle between scientific reason and religious superstition, an encounter that laid bare the tyranny of the Catholic Church.

However, the reality is that the charges brought against Galileo were largely motivated by fellow scientists and rivals, many of whom Galileo had insulted, bullied and dismissed in the years preceding the publication of his *Dialogue on the Two Great World Systems* (see p.135). Galileo's enemies – and there were many – set about to discredit the astronomer and successfully convinced Pope Urban VIII (a former friend and ally) that Galileo had within his *Dialogue* openly mocked the Pope's views about the universe.

In 1633 Galileo was accused of heresy and forced to stand trial. During the trial it was claimed that he had formerly been given an injunction by Cardinal Bellarmine in 1616, instructing him not to promote or teach the heliocentric theory (see p.135). Galileo rightly insisted that he'd never received such an injunction, only a private warning from Bellarmine not to 'hold' or 'defend' the view that the earth moved. In Galileo's view, the *Dialogue* did not contravene Bellarmine's warning as it presented both sides of the argument. The court eventually agreed not to press the most serious charge of 'violation of an injunction' as long as Galileo pleaded guilty to the charge that the *Dialogue* gave the impression that he was defending the heliocentric theory (although this hadn't been his intention).

In the end Galileo was convicted of the lesser charge of 'vehement suspicion of heresy', the court banned the *Dialogue* and Galileo was forced to formally recant his views. The details of his conviction were widely circulated, largely at the behest of Pope Urban VIII, who was keen to make an example of him. Within these documents (as shown by Maurice A. Finocchiaro in *Galileo Goes to Jail and Other Myths About Science and Religion*) we learn that Galileo was subjected to 'rigorous examination' during the interrogation process and that he was to be imprisoned for an indefinite period within the Inquisition jails in Rome. While torture was never mentioned, most assumed that 'rigorous examination' implied torture and that Galileo was indeed imprisoned in what many envisaged to be a miserable and dark cell.

However, the unearthing of documents in the eighteenth and nineteenth centuries show that Galileo's 'imprisonment', with the possible exception of three days in June 1633, consisted of lodging under house arrest in a number of rather grand houses around Italy, including the Tuscan Embassy and for a

GALILEO'S *DIALOGUE*

Released in 1632, Galileo's *Dialogue on the Two Great World Systems* debated the two conflicting theories on the order of the universe: the geocentric or Aristotelian view that the Earth is the centre of the universe (the basis of most European thought at that time); and the heliocentric or Copernican view that the Sun is the centre of the universe. In Galileo's *Dialogue*, the Copernican view, which appeared to contradict the Holy Scriptures (although Galileo was adamant that it didn't), not to speak of 'orthodox' scientific opinion of the day, ultimately won the debate. Whilst its publication caused considerable controversy within the Italian states, Galileo considered himself a good Catholic and believed that science and religion could be reconciled. In fact, prior to the *Dialogue* he had befriended several cardinals, including the man who became Pope Urban VIII, and dedicated his 1613 publication *Letters on Sunspots* to Pope Paul III. Indeed, prior to 1632 the Church largely accepted his science; it was the universities, steeped in the cosmology of Aristotle, who opposed him.

five-month period at the home of his good friend the Archbishop of Siena. Thereafter he resided at his own villa on house arrest, just outside Florence, until his death in 1642. The subsequent publication of documents relating to the trial (including minutes of an Inquisition meeting) in the late nineteenth century also revealed that it was highly unlikely that Galileo was tortured. It was rare for Inquisitors to torture defendants in Rome and rules forbade the torture of the elderly or the sick (Galileo was sixty-nine and suffering from arthritis and a hernia). Strict Inquisition rules also decreed that any torture had to be put to formal vote, of which there is again no reference. The worst that may have happened to Galileo is that he was *threatened* with torture; had he been physically tortured (which generally involved tying the victim's hands behind his back and suspending them from the ceiling, often resulting in dislocation of the shoulders) it's highly unlikely he would have been well enough to have attended the rest of the trial.

Galileo was a religious man who, despite his controversial scientific views, believed science and religion could be reconciled. Far from being persecuted by the Catholic Church, he was instead targeted by his fellow scientists, who were intent on discrediting his name. And whilst it was widely assumed that, following his conviction, Galileo was forced to live out his remaining days imprisoned in a dark cell, in truth he resided in his villa under a loosely enforced house arrest, where he would spend his time working on one of his finest works, the *Discourses on Two New Sciences*.

The Telescope

Galileo is generally credited as the inventor of the telescope. In fact, someone else came up with the idea, although sources vary on who this may have been. A popular candidate is the Dutch eyeglass-maker Hans Lippershey who in 1608 created a device consisting of two glasses in a tube that magnified distant objects. Others believe that, even earlier, Leonard Digges (*c.* 1515 to *c.* 1559), an English mathematician and father of the astronomer Thomas Digges, invented the first reflecting and refracting telescopes, although political circumstances prevented him capitalizing on his invention. Galileo substantially improved Lippershey's model (even though he hadn't actually seen it) and made a telescope with three times the magnification (and later thirty times the magnification). Using this more powerful telescope, Galileo was able to develop his revolutionary theories on astronomy, to include examining Jupiter and its orbiting four satellites (moons), which, he deduced, disproved the accepted geocentric view of cosmology.

Bloody Mary Was a Ruthless Persecutor of English Protestants

Mary I or 'Bloody Mary', as she is more commonly known, is remembered as a religious persecutor, a childless Tudor queen who mercilessly burnt at the stake hundreds, if not thousands, of Protestants in her quest to restore Catholicism in England. Mary did in fact execute 290 religious dissenters and Protestants, and while this was not an insignificant number for a five-year reign (1553–8), neither was it extraordinarily high when compared to the brutality of the times: Mary's sister Elizabeth I burnt just as many Catholics as Mary did Protestants, and their father Henry VIII killed off thousands more during his reign, especially during the religiously turbulent 1530s.

Mary I has remained, in the words of the historian Linda Porter, one of the 'most maligned and misunderstood of all monarchs'. Frequently depicted as a weak-willed Catholic bigot, her short reign has always compared unfavourably with the 'golden age' of Elizabeth I. As a woman and the first Queen of England it was thought she was already imbued with the 'feminine' traits of fierce emotion and unbridled lust, whereas Elizabeth triumphed because she showed more masculine traits, once famously proclaiming that though she had the 'body of a weak and feeble woman' she had the 'heart and stomach of a king'. Mary's Spanish heritage (her mother was Catherine of Aragon) and marriage to the Spanish king, Philip II, further entrenched her in the world of Catholicism and provoked deep suspicion among the English populace. Her desperate and failed attempts to produce a child proved her greatest tragedy and one that cast a gloomy shadow over her entire reign, undermining her marriage and ultimately leading to Protestant succession. And the loss of Calais during the Anglo-French War of 1557–9 resulted in national humiliation (whereas Elizabeth's defeat of the Spanish Armada led to national glory).

And yet when Mary was crowned Queen in 1553 there was jubilation amongst the populace as ballads, sermons and poems celebrated the arrival of a warrior queen and deliverer. In securing the throne, Mary had shown considerable determination and fortitude (far removed from her supposedly weak-willed nature), mustering men and support in East Anglia and the Thames Valley and causing the Privy Council to switch its allegiance from the incumbent Lady Jane Grey to Mary. Again, in 1554, Mary as Queen rallied Londoners with a rousing speech and blocked the entry of Thomas Wyatt and his army of rebels who were opposed to her intended marriage to Philip II. In an attempt to pacify the country and to dampen rumours that she was selling England to Spain, Mary proclaimed she was married to the realm first.

In July 1554 the royal marriage went ahead, whereupon Mary, who had initially shown some moderation towards her religious adversaries, pressed ahead with her plans to restore papal jurisdiction in England. In the autumn of that year, the heresy laws of the fifteenth century were revived (which allowed for burning as a penalty) and all of Henry VIII's statutes against papal authority were repealed. Around 800 Protestants, including the English historian John Foxe (see p.141), fled the country, whilst those who continued to defend their Protestant faith were subject to the heresy laws. The executions began with four clergymen in February 1555, and continued with the burning of Bishops Hugh Latimer and Nicholas Ridley, as well as the Archbishop of Canterbury, Thomas Cranmer, who, despite having recanted and repudiated Protestant theology, was condemned to death. With Cardinal Reginald Pole as Archbishop of Canterbury, the burnings continued, largely in the south-east and East Anglia, where Protestantism was more entrenched.

The common perception is that these executions, often known as the Marian Persecutions, turned its victims into martyrs of the Protestant cause, thus influencing public opinion against Catholicism and Mary's government. Eamon Duffy in his book *Fires of Faith* argues, however, that the burnings were largely accepted by the general populace. The real cause for growing discontent with Mary was her Spanish marriage, her pro-Spanish policies and war with France, which led to French forces seizing Calais, England's remaining foothold in Europe, in January 1558. Combined with this, the years of Mary's reign were also persistently wet, which resulted in failed harvests and famine, despite the attempts of Mary and her council to provide relief for the starving.

The Origins of the Bloody Mary Myth

The maligning of Mary's image began as soon as Elizabeth I took the throne and gained momentum in the seventeenth century, when Protestants, who nicknamed her 'Bloody Mary', used her example to highlight the dangers of Catholic rule in England. The perception of Mary as a brutal tyrant was largely shaped by two publications written by the Protestant exiles John Knox and John Foxe. Knox's *The First Blast of the Trumpet Against the Monstrous Regiment of Women,* published in 1558, attacked Mary and referred to her as a 'monstrous Amazona'. And John Foxe's *The Book of Martyrs*, published in 1563, 'recorded in loving and gruesome detail' the lives and deaths of Mary's victims. The book went on to be a bestseller, and was read almost as widely as the Bible. As Roger Lockyer in *Tudor and Stuart Britain 1471–1714* states, 'Mary had given the English Protestant church its martyrs; Foxe made sure that their deeds would be an inspiration to generations of those who came after.'

The reign of Mary I is now inextricably linked with the persecution of Protestants, yet in the 1550s thousands of Protestants in the Netherlands lost their lives and far more Huguenot Protestants were burnt in France (culminating in the infamous St Bartholomew's Day Massacre of 1572 when anything between 5,000 and 10,000 were killed). The obsession with the Marian Persecutions also tends to overlook Mary's achievements as monarch: she improved the financial administration of government (which had been sliding towards bankruptcy during the years of Henry VIII); she reformed the coinage; managed Parliament; and ultimately secured the throne as the first crowned Queen of England and Ireland (thereby defending the line of Tudor succession).

Mary's greatest misfortune was to die young (from fever at the age of forty-two) and childless – had she lived longer and succeeded in re-establishing Catholicism, she no doubt would have been celebrated as a valiant defender of the nation's faith. Instead, her history was written by Protestants, who bequeathed to us the image of Mary as a ruthless persecutor of Protestants, an image that, however distorted, is still as prevalent today as it was in the days of John Foxe.

St Patrick Was Irish

On St Patrick's Day (17 March) millions of people around the world dress in green, don a shamrock and celebrate all things Irish. As the patron saint of Ireland, the fifth-century apostle of St Patrick is seen as the very embodiment of Ireland and a true Irishman in every sense. However, he was in fact born in Britain, his original name was Maewyn Succat and he didn't go to Ireland until the age of sixteen.

Two letters written in Latin, which are generally accepted to have been written by St Patrick, provide the only detail we have on the apostle's life. He was born in (or around) AD 387 to a Romanized British family in, as he tells us in *Confessio*, the settlement of 'Bannavem Taburniae'. This place name now does not exist on any current map of Britain, although locations suggested include Kilpatrick in Scotland, Banwen in Wales and somewhere between Chester and the Solway Firth.

Patrick tells us that when he was sixteen he was captured by a gang of Irish pirates and taken as a slave to Ireland. There he spent six years herding sheep and tending pigs, again at an uncertain location, possibly in County Mayo or at Slemish Mountain in County Antrim. It was during these years that 'he turned with fervour to his faith' and spent much of his time praying.

Patrick finally managed to escape captivity in Ireland by stowing away on a boat bound for Britain, and he eventually returned to live with his parents. Having been trained and ordained a priest, he returned to Ireland in AD 432 inspired, as he wrote in *Confessio*, to go back in a dream by a voice that said to him (as translated from the Latin), 'We beg you, holy youth, that you shall come and shall walk again among us.'

He answered his calling and returned to Ireland as the country's second bishop. Now known as Patrick, he went on to baptize and convert thousands of people and bring the message of Christianity to much of Ireland. However, Patrick was probably not Ireland's first Christian missionary, as it's likely there were already other Christian believers in the country. Ireland had strong trading links with the Roman Empire and therefore would have been touched by Christianity in some way. In the fifth century Pope Celestine I is said to have sent Ireland its first bishop, Palladius, and he may well have joined other clerics already administering to existing Christian communities in Ireland.

Following a fairly turbulent life as a bishop in Ireland (during which time he was robbed, arrested and accused of financial impropriety), Patrick died (it is said) on 17 March AD 461 (although AD 493 has also been suggested). Thereon he was largely forgotten, although mythology slowly grew around the legend of Patrick during the twelfth century. Centuries later, as part of the widespread veneration of saints and missionaries – particularly Irish ones – who continued to spread Christianity, monastic and scholarly traditions when the rest of Europe had fallen to warring tribes, Patrick was honoured as the patron saint of Ireland.

Saint Patrick's feast day has been observed in Ireland as a fairly minor religious holiday for centuries. In the main, it's Irish immigrants living abroad, particularly those living in the US, who, in a bid to reconnect with their Irish roots, have turned St Patrick's Day into a much bigger celebration. The first St Patrick's Day parades were held by Irish soldiers fighting in the American War of Independence and hundreds of parades and celebrations are now held in the US, Canada, Australia and across the world. In Ireland, St Patrick's Day has also become more commercialized (up until the 1970s all pubs in Ireland were closed on St Patrick Day) and hundreds of thousands of people now take part in Dublin's multi-day celebrations.

So the truth is out: St Patrick was not Irish, nor did he alone establish Christianity in Ireland. But perhaps the old adage that 'everybody's Irish on St Patrick's Day' applies just as much to St Patrick as it does to those celebrating his memory.

ST PATRICK AND THE SNAKES

Another popular myth associated with St Patrick is that
he freed Ireland from snakes by driving them into the sea
after they began attacking him during a forty-day fast.
According to the *Concise Oxford Dictionary of the Christian
Church*, 'he stood on a hill ... and used a staff to herd
the slithering creatures into the sea, banishing them for
eternity.' The problem with this myth is that snakes have
never existed in Ireland, and still don't today. Following the
last Ice Age 10,000 years ago, snakes returned to northern
and western Europe, but never returned to Ireland as it was
protected by the surrounding seas. (In fact, Ireland, along
with Greenland, Iceland, New Zealand and Antarctica, are
the few places in the world which are completely snake-free
zones.) The story has a more metaphorical meaning: snakes
often symbolize evil and the driving out of the snakes more
likely refers to Patrick's mission to rid Ireland of its
evil, pagan influence.

ROMAN GLADIATORS FOUGHT TO THE DEATH

It's a popular belief that the citizens of Ancient Rome liked to spend much of their year perched high up in the amphitheatre, where they could revel in the bloodbath of the gladiatorial contests below. Gladiators fighting to the death or slaying an array of exotic animals provided a captivating spectacle – and an image of Roman brutality that still holds great fascination today. Yet the reality of gladiatorial contests was quite different from this common perception: combat developed during the Roman period from a funeral rite and fight to the death to a highly organized public spectacle in which the death of the gladiator was no longer the ultimate goal.

Indeed, much of what we know (or think we know) about gladiatorial combat is mired in misconception, shaped in relatively recent years by the Hollywood blockbusters *Spartacus* (1960) and *Gladiator* (2000). It's an area of history often subject to vivid imaginings and supposition as little survives from the period to tell us exactly what happened during gladiatorial games. Contemporary accounts, written histories, Roman mosaics and other pictorial images give some background clues, but written descriptions of actual gladiatorial matches are few and far between (see p.149).

DE SPECTACULIS

The only surviving detailed account of a gladiatorial battle comes from the Roman poet Martial. The poem, from his *De spectaculis*, describes a battle between the gladiators Verus and Priscus held in AD 80, on the first day of Emperor Titus's games at the Colosseum in Rome. It's an evenly matched fight ('equal they fought, equal they yielded'), both are declared victors and both are granted the *rudis*, or wooden sword, by Titus which signified their freedom.

The gladiatorial games, during which armed combatants ('gladiators', meaning 'swordsmen') fought against each other, evolved from an Etruscan funeral rite in which the dead were honoured with offerings of blood. These *munera,* as they were called, were believed to have been introduced to Rome in 216 BC when the sons of Marcus Lepidus honoured their deceased father by setting three pairs of gladiators against each other in a fight to the death. In 46 BC Julius Caesar, having commemorated his father in a similar away, hosted a *munera* at the tomb of his daughter Julia, who had died in childhood eight years previously. An elaborate affair (which included the first appearance of a giraffe), large numbers, including several of Caesar's own soldiers, were killed.

Gradually the *munera* became separated from the funerary context, and evolved into a very public display of wealth and prestige by the aristocratic elite. In Rome the emperors eventually assumed control of the 'gladiatorial games' and by the time of Trajan (AD 98–117) military victories were celebrated by as many as 5,000 pairs of gladiators. By the end of the second century AD Tertullian in *De spectaculis* (XII) complained that 'this class of public entertainment has passed from being a compliment to the dead to being a compliment to the living'.

For these more public spectacles, gladiators were no longer required to fight to the death (unlike the more private *munera*, for which death was a necessary outcome). The running order of events at these gladiatorial games often followed a standard formula: animal fights or hunts in the morning (usually fought not by gladiators as such but by condemned criminals known as *bestiarii* or by trained animal hunters known as *venatores*); then a variety of special features, which could include the execution of criminals or 'comedy fights'; followed by the gladiatorial contests in the afternoon.

THUMBS UP / THUMBS DOWN

It's popularly thought that Roman spectators would decide the fate of a defeated gladiator by showing either a 'thumbs down' for death, or 'thumbs up' if they thought he should be spared. However, one of the only direct references to this hand gesture comes from the Roman poet Juvenal, who wrote in his *Satire III* that the Roman mob indicated who should be slain by 'a turn of the thumb'. The problem is we don't know which way the thumb was turned: some historians claim it was turned upwards, others downwards or in a sideways motion. And there is little evidence to corroborate Juvenal's reference (Martial wrote that a crowd appealed for mercy by waving a handkerchief or by shouting). If a gladiator wished to surrender, it's thought that he would lay down his arms and raise his index finger, usually on the left hand, as a gesture of mercy to the crowd. The referee would then stop the match and would refer to the editor or emperor if a final decision needed to be made.

The main sponsor of the games was known as the 'editor' and many matches employed a senior referee and an assistant (as depicted in many mosaics featuring gladiatorial combat). These referees would keep a close eye on the proceedings, whilst deferring to the judgement of the editor, who could decide the fate of a defeated combatant (based largely on the mood of the crowd). While the exact details surrounding the rules of combats are lost, the existence of these mediators suggests the matches were well organized and subject to complex regulations.

It's thought that the combatants, rather than fighting each other in a great free-for-all, more commonly fought in evenly matched pairs, with one style of gladiator pitted against another (there were seven categories of fighters). A *retarius* gladiator, for example, who was lightly armed with a net and trident, might be paired with the more heavily armed, but less mobile, *secutor*. These gladiators, who were mostly slaves, prisoners of war and the occasional free-born volunteer, received rigorous training, lots of food and medical attention and were thus viewed by their trainers (*lanistae*) as valuable commodities, not to be despatched lightly. The top gladiators might fight only two or three times a year, and some gladiators survived to reach retirement. If a gladiator died during combat, a *lanista* might well expect the game's editor to pay heavy compensation, thus making any gladiatorial bloodbath an expensive outcome for the game organizers.

It's been estimated that during the first century AD there was a 90 per cent survival rate among gladiators. In a society where life and death hung in precarious balance, where half of Rome's population would die before their twentieth birthday, the professional gladiator, fighting for the entertainment of the masses, would fare much better than many of his spectators. So, while death was a certainty for any condemned criminals who entered the arena, few bouts – probably a maximum of one in ten – ended in the death of a gladiator.

The idea that Roman gladiators fought to the death has been propounded throughout history, and has been more recently popularized with the release of gladiator-themed Hollywood blockbusters. Yet, while historical evidence of actual combat is scarce, what does survive challenges the common perception that gladiators fought to the death for the sport evolved into an organized spectacle, and gladiators highly trained and invaluable commodities.

VICHY FRANCE LEADER PHILIPPE PÉTAIN TRIED TO SAVE JEWS FROM THE HOLOCAUST

Set up after the German invasion of France, the Vichy Government of 1940–5 was headed by the First World War veteran Marshal Philippe Pétain. As a collaborative government, Pétain's administration maintained legal authority over roughly two-fifths of France, with the capital situated in the central spa town of Vichy. By 1939 France had the second biggest population of Jews in Europe (some 330,000), half of whom were European refugees who had gone to France in the hope that they would be protected from persecution. However, between 1942 and 1945 the Vichy regime transported nearly 76,000 Jewish refugees and French citizens to Nazi concentration camps. Pétain always claimed he opposed their deportation, and that he had in fact tried everything he could to stop it, but increasing evidence has come to light to suggest he and other Vichy officials were fully complicit in the deportation.

The image of Pétain as reluctant Nazi collaborator and innocent bystander during the Holocaust persisted in France for over half a century, much of it borne from a general unwillingness to revisit the 'dark years' of the Vichy regime. For decades, common perception had it that the Vichy government shielded the French from the worst evils of Nazi rule, an argument reinforced by Robert Aron in his major 1954 historical work *Histoire de Vichy*. The popular view was that Pétain, the great hero of the First World War's Verdun, skilfully played off the Germans while in secret negotiations with the Allies, and it was his pro-Nazi Prime Minister Pierre Laval ('the Germans' man') who was largely to blame for the anti-Jewish sentiment within Vichy.

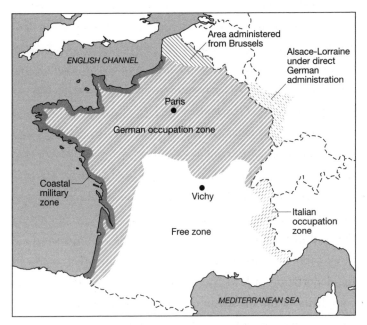

A map of Vichy France, 1940–4

But in 1972 the publication of a book by American historian Robert Paxton, *Vichy France: Old Guard and New Order 1940–1944*, demolished this image of the Vichy regime, reigniting a bitter debate in France. Having examined both French and German records, Paxton showed that Pétain wasn't playing any sort of double game with the Nazis, that the Germans in fact gave Pétain enormous freedom of action, and that the Vichy regime's ultimate aim was to establish itself within the Nazi new order of France.

In 1981 another book by Paxton and Michael Marrus, *Vichy France and the Jews*, argued that anti-Semitism was at the very heart of the Vichy regime and that Vichy officials and police were directly involved in the rounding up of Jews to the east. Six years later, in 1983, the bringing to trial of Klaus Barbie, the German chief of the Gestapo in Lyon, further highlighted the involvement of the Vichy regime in the Holocaust, as did the jailing of one of his French aides, Paul Touvier, in 1992. It wasn't until 1995 that Jacques Chirac, who had succeeded ex-Vichy official Francois Mitterand as president of France, apologized to the Jews for 'the criminal insanity of the occupying power [that] was assisted by [the] French State', breaking with the long-standing conviction that Vichy was an illegal aberration that did not represent France. And the 1998 imprisonment of ex-cabinet minister Maurice Papon for his involvement in the deportation of Jews from Bordeaux finally established the complicity of the French in the Holocaust. Since then, France has paid compensation and returned property to survivors, and opened up a wealth of previously undisclosed archives relating to the Vichy government.

In 2010, the anonymous donation of a previously unseen document to the Holocaust Memorial Museum in Paris provided an unsettling insight into the first anti-Jewish legislation of the Vichy regime. Enacted in October 1940, the statute excluded

Jews from a wide range of professions, leading to the confiscation of Jewish property and a broad system of anti-Semitic measures that later facilitated the holding and deportation of Jews to Nazi death camps. Throughout 1940 and 1941 more than 40,000 refugees were held in French concentration camps, while in 1941 French police began mass arrests of Jewish people. In August 1942 Vichy police hunted down Jewish refugees, seized Jewish families from their homes and transported around 11,000 men, women and children to the Drancy internment camp outside Paris (a main transit centre for Auschwitz). During 1942 Vichy officials sent 41,951 Jews to Germany, then another 31,889 in 1943 and 1944. Out of 75,721 Jewish deportees, fewer than 2,000 survived.

Part of the draft bill for the 1940 anti-Jewish legislation, the newly donated document contained numerous annotations that experts have authenticated as Pétain's own handwriting. The document reveals that the statute originally excluded the descendants of Jews who were born French or naturalized before 1860. Pétain's alleged amendments crossed out the exclusion clause and made the statute applicable to all Jews, both foreign and French, and barred them from a wider range of professions. The historian and lawyer Serge Klarsfeld, who unveiled the document, said, 'This document establishes Pétain's decisive role in drawing up this position in the most aggressive way,' indicating that Laval was not solely responsible for the regime's anti-Semitic measures. It also destroys the still widely held myth that Pétain and the Vichy regime sought to protect French Jews over refugee Jews (as at least double the percentage of non-

French Jews died between 1940 and 1944 as compared to 15 per cent of French Jews).

Right from the outset of the Vichy regime, it's clear that Pétain never had any intention to save Jews, French or otherwise, from deportation. Moreover, as Klarsfeld says, 'Pétain not only intervened to push legislation against Jews further than proposed, but created an entire anti-Semitic outlook and framework that in 1940 was even harsher than what the Germans had adopted.' The unveiling of this document marks another major step in history's re-examination of Pétain, further demolishing the now dwindling argument that he strove to protect Jews living in France from the Holocaust.

Thanksgiving Day in the US Harks Back to the 'First Thanksgiving' Given by Plymouth Settlers in 1621

In the USA, Thanksgiving Day, held on the fourth Thursday in November, is a time for families to feast, watch football or take in a parade, and to give thanks, of course, for the many blessings of the past year. The common assumption is that the celebration owes its origins to the 'first Thanksgiving' of 1621, when New England settlers in Plymouth gave thanks to God for a bountiful harvest following a particularly harsh winter (during which 46 of the 102 pilgrims died). According to the only contemporary account we have of the event, written by the Pilgrim leader Edward Winslow in *Mourt's Relation*, feasting and recreation took place over three days and were shared with ninety Wampanoag Indians and their chief Massasoit, who donated five deer to the celebrations.

The origins of Thanksgiving, however, are not quite so clear-cut and, like many commonly accepted traditions, are a blurring of myth and fact. To begin with, the events of 1621 did not technically constitute the 'first Thanksgiving'. Celebrations to give thanks for a good harvest or any kind of good fortune is a ritual common to cultures all around the world, and they were certainly performed in America before 1621. Indeed, for millennia Native Americans have performed rituals giving thanks for all the gifts of life. Settlers in Newfoundland in 1578 probably held one of the first colonial services of Thanksgiving (a combination of age-old traditions of harvest festivals with religious services), as had the Spanish settlers in Florida some years before that.

You realize this means we'll have to invite them back to our place.

Support for the Thanksgiving ceremony did start to gain some ground following the feast of 1621. In 1623 the Plymouth settlers held a Thanksgiving service even greater than the ceremony they'd held two years previously, after their prayers during a drought led to some much-needed rain. Governor Bradford proclaimed it a day of Thanksgiving in the form of prayers and thanks to God. Thereon, the occasional day of Thanksgiving, in the form of prayers for military victories or any kind of auspicious event, was held, albeit sporadically and at a very local level.

A COVER-UP JOB

Neither the Wampanoag Indians nor the British settlers referred to the harvest feast of 1621 as a 'Thanksgiving'. Some theorists have suggested that the three-day event was more likely a series of political meetings to secure a military alliance. Neither side trusted each other fully and the arrival of ninety American Indians (all of them men) following the sound of gunshot from the British hunters was probably an act of military precaution.

For many Native Americans, Thanksgiving represents the conquest and genocide of their people, and some have accused the United States of fabricating the Thanksgiving story in a bid to whitewash the injustice caused to the indigenous people of America.

It wasn't until 1777 that regular Thanksgiving ceremonies took place, when the Continental Congress declared the first national day of Thanksgiving (largely in response to the defeat of the British at Saratoga during the American War of Independence). Later in the century, various congressional representatives pushed for the adoption of a legal holiday of Thanksgiving but questions were raised over its legitimacy and date. Presidents Washington, Adams and Monroe issued further proclamations for days of national Thanksgivings, although Presidents Jefferson and Jackson objected to the national government's involvement in a religious observance.

By the 1850s most states celebrated Thanksgiving but often on different dates.

President Abraham Lincoln, in the midst of the Civil War, was the first to declare Thanksgiving a national holiday in the hope it might unite a war-torn country. The date Lincoln chose was 6 August, although it was moved arbitrarily to the last Thursday of November the following year. (And here it has roughly remained, bar a two-year interlude during the Depression when Franklin D. Roosevelt brought it forward by a week in a bid to lengthen the Christmas shopping season.)

It wasn't until the late nineteenth century that Thanksgiving became particularly associated with the harvest celebration of 1621. The establishment of the national holiday of Thanksgiving coincided with a renewed interest in the Pilgrims and the Wampanoag, caused partly by the recovery of the lost manuscript *Of Plimoth Plantation* by Governor Bradford (a retrospective journal describing the early days of the Plymouth colony) in 1855, along with Henry Wadsworth Longfellow's poem *The Courtship of Miles Standish* in 1858. The idea was further entrenched by the antiquarian Alexander Young, who commented in 1841 when he published the pilgrim leader Edward Winslow's previously lost account of the harvest meal of 1621, 'This was the first Thanksgiving, the harvest festival of New England.'

By the beginning of the twentieth century the harvest meal of 1621 had begun to be taught to school children to teach them about being good citizens (and is still lovingly recreated and sung about in school plays and pageants across the nation). At the same time, the holiday moved away from its religious roots, enabling immigrants in the US to share in its tradition, while the more secular traditions of parades and sporting events grew in number.

TURKEY DINNER

The modern-day Thanksgiving meal of turkey, sweet potato pie, corn bread, mashed potato, berries, cranberry sauce and pumpkin pie is said to resemble the harvest meal of 1621. However, turkey was not specifically mentioned in Edward Winslow's account, who wrote, '… Our governor sent four men on fowling … They four in one day killed as much fowl as, with a little help beside, served the company almost a week.' Whilst the settlers and Wampanoag ate wild turkey, at that time of year (the harvest meal was held at some point between the beginning of October and beginning of November), it's likely they hunted waterfowl, such as duck or goose. The 1621 feast also included venison as Winslow mentions the Wampanoag donating five deer, and it's doubtful the settlers would have had the sugar they needed to make cranberry sauce or pumpkin pie (although they may well have had pumpkins). Berries and other fresh fruits would also have been out of season.

Thanksgiving Day still has a deep association with the events of 1621, and in doing so has come to symbolize intercultural peace and the sanctity of home, family and the community. But it wasn't until the late nineteenth century that this association really took root. The combination of Lincoln's declaration of Thanksgiving as a national holiday, and the rediscovery of lost manuscripts relating to the Plymouth settlers, consolidated the idea that Thanksgiving harked back to the harvest meal of 1621.

Oliver Cromwell:
Man of the People and
Common-Man's Hero

In 1653 Oliver Cromwell (1599–1658) rose from provincial obscurity to become Lord Protector of England, Scotland and Ireland and ruler of the nation's republican Commonwealth. A revolutionary figure who rallied for the abolition of monarchy, Cromwell has gained the reputation of a common-man's hero, a man who, in opposition to aristocratic and monarchial oppression, rose from nowhere to become the most powerful man in England. And yet Cromwell hailed from aristocratic stock, and his ancestry was anything but common.

Blacker is the new black.

In 1599 Cromwell was born into a considerably wealthy family in Huntingdonshire, several members of whom had served as JPs or MPs for the county. While Cromwell's family had no hereditary title – and his position as the eldest son of the younger son of a knight was considered to be socially ambiguous – various other male members of his family had also been knighted and the family could even trace its lineage back to the great Tudor dynasty, of which Cromwell was a direct descendant. Cromwell's great-grandfather was a Welshman named Morgan ap Williams, who married Catherine Cromwell, the elder sister of Thomas Cromwell (Henry VIII's chief minister). Rather than keeping the Welsh name of Williams – which, strictly speaking, should have been Oliver Cromwell's surname – the family chose to keep the name of Cromwell, in honour of their distinguished relative. Morgan ap Williams was the grandson (by illegitimate birth) of Jasper Tudor, who was uncle to the Tudor monarch Henry VII and the son of Owen Tudor, the founder of the Tudor dynasty and husband to the daughter of Charles VI of France, Catherine of Valois. Therefore Oliver Cromwell's illustrious ancestry may well have included not just the House of Tudor but also some of the great dynasties of Europe.

Cromwell's own father, the JP Robert Cromwell, had served as a Member of Parliament under Elizabeth I. When he died, Oliver was forced to take charge of the family at the age of eighteen, looking after his widowed mother and seven unmarried sisters and, from 1620, his own wife and growing family. It was at this point that Cromwell's social standing dipped slightly. His annual income of £100 a year was just enough for him to retain his gentleman status, although by 1631 he was forced to move to St Ives, East Anglia, where he lived as a tenant farmer, dressing in plain russet like the other yeomen. But this sharp decline in his social and financial standing was relatively short-lived, as by 1636 he had inherited the control of various properties from his maternal uncle, Sir Thomas Steward, which increased his income to £300 a year and restored him once again to the standing of a gentleman.

Despite his momentary dip in fortunes, Cromwell remained exceptionally well connected, which played a vital part in his later political and military career. Between 1628 and 1629, he served as MP for Huntingdon (although he only gave one, badly received, speech) alongside eight of his cousins in Parliament, and many of his relatives served in the later Long Parliament, including his cousins John Hampden and Oliver St John. His marriage to Elizabeth Bourchier, daughter of the London merchant and landowner Sir James Bourchier, had also brought Cromwell into contact with a number of leading Puritan families, as well as the London merchant community and the Earls of Warwick and Holland.

In around 1628, Cromwell suffered illness and depression, which led to a profound spiritual awakening that left him with strong and uncompromising Puritan beliefs. In 1640 Cromwell returned to both the Long and Short Parliaments as MP for Cambridge, a position he likely secured through means of his influential contacts (for he was almost certainly the least well-off man there). He is said to have arrived in Parliament shabbily dressed in a poorly tailored 'plain cloth suit', his neckband splattered in blood. He was known for his passionate manner in Parliament, dropping 'tears down with his words', seeming to lack the finesse and polish of some of his parliamentary colleagues. However, although Cromwell may have looked to some like a country bumpkin, much of it was borne from his religious convictions, which advocated plain dress and less emphasis on outward appearance.

CROMWELL AS LORD PROTECTOR

The nature of Cromwell's role as head of the Commonwealth was revolutionary, but his aim was never to reform the social order or to extend the rights of the common man. After the turmoil of the Civil War, his ambition as Lord Protector was to restore a stable government, and to promote freedom of worship and godliness through spiritual and moral reform. Cromwell had nothing against hierarchy in state or society, proclaiming, 'a nobleman, a gentleman, a yeoman, the distinction of these: that is a good interest of the nation, and a great one!' He considered the beliefs of the Levellers, which included extending the suffrage and equality before law, tantamount to anarchy. In essence, his views were those of a country gentleman, in keeping with the beliefs of his parliamentary colleagues and kinsmen.

Cromwell's successful military career (1643–1651) – when, with no previous experience as a military captain, he was promoted first to colonel and then to senior officer in six heartland counties for parliamentarianism – during the Civil War radically improved his financial circumstances. As early as 1641–2 he was able to pledge quite large sums towards reconquering Ireland (between £1,200 to £2,000) and his military salary combined with the granting of extensive lands across England led to a considerable fortune of well in excess of £10,000 per annum. As Lord Protector (1553–8) his standing as the most powerful man in England brought him even greater personal wealth.

Cromwell's rise, particularly in the context of the seventeenth century, was indeed meteoric, and his style of government revolutionary in that there were hints of something approaching democracy. While for a short time his position dipped below that of a gentleman, and his religious convictions insisted on a more basic style of dress, his family lineage, with its strong links to the gentry and aristocracy, suggested Cromwell was far from the common-man's hero of historical myth. Not only was he related to a distinguished Tudor statesman, but, as a descendant through the male line of Owen, he was also a member of the great Tudor dynasty itself.

The US Army Defeated the Japanese and Liberated Vietnam in 1945

In 1945 Vietnam formed part of French Indochina, but it had been occupied by Japan throughout Second World War. In March 1945 Japan consolidated its rule of the country when it completely ousted the Vichy French and installed Emperor Bao Dai at the helm of the newly entitled Empire of Vietnam. But Japan's rule was brief and unstable, and her surrender quickly followed in August of that year. Yet rather than the US leading the defeat, it was actually the Vietnamese who led the resistance movement and forced the Japanese to surrender, whereupon America and her allies thwarted Vietnam's desire for independence by handing back control of the country to the French.

Disaster for France in the early stages of the Second World War had significant repercussions for the country's hold over its colonies. And Vietnam, geographically remote from the West and governed by the French since the late nineteenth century (see p.173), became an easy target for Japan, which sought to take advantage of French weakness and extend its sphere of influence in South-East Asia. During the Second World War the US – which, up until the last four months of fighting, was still under the guidance of the ostensibly anti-colonial Roosevelt – and its allies had been complicit in Japan's endeavours. They were at that stage sceptical of French control over Vietnam and encouraged

France to accept Japan's usurpation. As Bernard B. Fall outlines in *Street Without Joy*, France's decision to sign the non-aggression pact with Thailand (Japan's ally) in 1940 indicated collaboration on France's behalf. And thus Japan's decisive attack on 9 March 1945 to capture any remaining French troops in Vietnam went uncontested by the Allies.

Both France and Vietnam made immediate moves to contest Japan's takeover. While General de Gaulle's declaration of 24 March 1945, which stated its intention to establish an independent regime in Vietnam and the rest of Indochina (see p.173), while maintaining its own sovereignty, went largely unheeded, charismatic Communist leader Ho Chi Minh and his national independence front, the Viet Minh, emerged as a strong nationalist presence which sought to gain independence for Vietnam. The group had formed in 1941 and had steadily built up support by planting Communists throughout the country to try and gain followers. And, as Bernard B. Fall notes, their Communist training 'gave them an unbeatable headstart over the small idealistic nationalist groups which began to squabble over details while the Communists were taking over the country under their noses.'

The Allies hadn't reckoned on the Vietnamese spirit of independence and were initially slow to intercept – US General Douglas MacArthur forbade reoccupation of Vietnam until he received Japanese surrender in Tokyo, which wasn't due until 2 September 1945. This dithering meant the path was clear for the Vietnamese to take control. During the August Revolution of 1945 Ho Chi Minh and the Viet Minh forced the Japanese to surrender and they seized power in Hanoi. On 2 September Ho Chi Minh issued the Proclamation of Independence of the Democratic Republic of Vietnam and convinced Emperor Bao Dai to abdicate. As Pierre Brocheux and Daniel Hémery state in *Indochina: An Ambiguous Colonization: 1858–1954*, following Japanese surrender, Indochina found itself 'in a state of moral and political secession from France' and Ho Chi Minh and the Viet Minh were the best equipped to cope.

However, the world failed to cooperate and Ho Chi Minh's government went unrecognized, despite repeated petitions to the US President Harry Truman asking for his support. And despite their strength in numbers, the Viet Minh were ultimately hampered by their lack of resources, which left them unable to take full advantage of the situation – they had no military, financial or governmental power and failed to establish effective military control following Japan's surrender.

And whilst Roosevelt had been hostile to French colonization, his demise and Harry Truman's accession in April 1945 put a decisive end to such a stance. At the Potsdam Conference in July 1945 the Allies accepted the re-establishment of French troops in Indochina; the British were entrusted with the disarmament of Japanese troops south of the 16th Parallel and the rearmament of French troops. The spirit of colonialism was reawakened – at least in the eyes of the Allies – as France was once again seen as the rightful administrator of Indochina. Brocheux and Hémery believe America's increasing support of France's recolonization of Indochina was a result of the threat the Soviet Union posed and the importance of France in an international context. On 5 October 1945 a telegram from the Secretary of State Dean Acheson confirmed US approval of the return of Indochina to the French, and the head of the OSS William Donovan reiterated this stance when he stated it was necessary for Europe to maintain its empire in the face of Communism. France began its reconquest.

Vietnam's dreams of independence had been thwarted. The British finally left in March 1946 and handed control over to the French. But the Vietnamese nationalist spirit remained strong, and on 19 December 1946 the Viet Minh initiated the First Indochina War against the French. The war in Vietnam, which would last until 1954, had begun. And it wasn't until the end of this war, following the French defeat at Dien Bien Phu, that France's colonial grip on Vietnam was finally dissolved. However, years of fighting divided the country, with Ho Chi Minh's Communist Democratic Republic of Vietnam situated in the north, and Ngo Dinh Diem's State of Vietnam in the south. Ho Chi Minh's instigation of a guerrilla campaign against the south in the late 1950s sparked off the Vietnam War, and it wasn't until July 1976 that the north and south of the country were finally united to form the Socialist Republic of Vietnam, following years of horrific bloodshed.

Ho Chi Minh and the Viet Minh were responsible for defeating the Japanese in 1945. When the Japanese had invaded Vietnam, France's colonial grip had been very much on the wane and Vietnam's desire for independence was growing exponentially. But the decision of the US and Allies to intervene and reinstate French colonial control only served to prolong the efforts of the Vietnamese to attain independence. Real and long-lasting independence wasn't achieved until well into the 1970s, after the North Vietnamese victory over South Vietnam and it's American ally. By the time of his death in 1969 Ho Chi Minh had not only defeated the Japanese, but the French, the South Vietnamese and the Americans too.

A Brief History of French Indochina

France established its colonial conquest of Indochina in 1887 when a federation of the three Vietnamese regions of Tonkin (north), Annam (central) and Cochinchina (south) and Cambodia was formed. Laos was added in 1893, and Kouang-Tchéou-Wan (a region on the south coast of China) in 1900. As Brocheux and Hémery state, the Second World War sounded the death knell of the old European empires, and France could only watch on in horror as first the Japanese and then the Vietnamese sought to take control. In 1949 Cambodia and Laos were both granted autonomy under the French Union and their monarchies remained.

But Vietnam, which was the most politically dynamic country of all Indochina and with the best resources, came under sustained external attack. France's colonial grip on Indochina was finally halted with the proclamation of the Geneva Agreements in April 1954, which supported the territorial integrity of Indochina and declared the cessation of hostilities and foreign involvement in the region.

BIBLIOGRAPHY

BIBLIOGRAPHY

1415: Henry V's Year of Glory by Ian Mortimer (Vintage)

America: Empire of Liberty by David Reynolds (Penguin)

At Home: A Short History of Private Life by Bill Bryson (Doubleday)

Australia: A Biography of a Nation by Phillip Knightley (Vintage)

Blood Lands: Europe Between Hitler and Stalin by Timothy Snyder (Bodley Head)

A Century of Troubles England 1600–1700 by Stevie Davies (Pan Macmillan)

Debunking History: 152 Popular Myths Exploded by Ed Rayner and Ron Stapley (Sutton)

England and Wales under the Tudors by Sinclair Atkins (Hodder Arnold)

The Family, Sex and Marriage in England 1500–1800 by Lawrence Stone (Penguin)

Galileo Goes to Jail and Other Myths About Science and Religion edited by Ronald L. Numbers (Harvard University Press)

History's Greatest Lies by William Weir (Fair Winds)

Indochina: An Ambiguous Colonization 1858-1954 by Pierre Brocheux and Daniel Hémery (University of California Press)

Lenin: A Biography by Robert Service (Macmillan)

Lies, Damned Lies and History by Graeme Donald (The History Press)

Made in America by Bill Bryson (Minerva)

Mao's Great Famine: The History of China's Most Devastating Catastrophe 1958–62 by Frank Dikötter (Bloomsbury)

Mud, Blood and Poppycock by Gordon Corrigan (Cassell)

The New Penguin Dictionary of Modern History 1789–1945 (Penguin)

Not So! Popular Myths About America from Columbus to Clinton by Paul F. Boller Jr. (Oxford University Press)

Oxford Dictionary of World History (Oxford University Press)

Queen Elizabeth's Wooden Teeth and other Historical Fallacies by Andrea Barham (Michael O'Mara)

Race for the South Pole – The Expedition Diaries of Scott and Amundsen by Roland Huntford (Continuum)

Street Without Joy by Bernard B. Fall (Stackpole Books)

Tudor and Stuart Britain 1471–1714 by Roger Lockyer (Longman)

Who Was Mr Nobody? Debunking Historical Mysteries by Ed Rayner and Ron Stapley (Sutton)

UnRoman Britain: Exposing the Great Myth of Britannia by Miles Russell and Stuart Laycock (The History Press)

ARTICLES AND WEBSITES

'The Madness of King George III: a Psychiatric Re-Assessment' by Timothy J. Peters and Allan Beveridge, *History of Psychiatry*, 1 March 2010, vol. twenty-one, hpy.sagepub.com/content/21/1/20

'Roman Britain to Anglo-Saxon England', *History Today*, 30

September 1990, historytoday.com/Catherine-hills/roman-britain-anglo-saxon-england

'Inventing the Iron Chancellor' by Robert Gerwarth, *History Today*, June 2001

Archaeology.co.uk

Archaeology.org

Australianhistoryresearch.info

BBC *History* Magazine – historyextra.com

Bbc.co.uk/history

Forum.stirpes.net/revisionism/8495-top-10-myths-about-spanish-armada.html

France24.com

Guardian.co.uk

History Today historytoday.com

Independent.co.uk

Literaryreview.co.uk

Mgsanchez.net/2008/08/writing-myth-monumentalism-and.html

News.nationalgeographic.com

Nytimes.com

Olivercromwell.org

Penelope.uchicago.edu/encyclopedia_romana/gladiators

Plimoth.org/learn/thanksgiving-history

Si.edu/Encyclopedia_SI/nmah/thanks

Telegraph.co.uk

Thesundaytimes.co.uk

Time.com

Wikipedia

INDEX

This index is compiled on a word-by-word basis rather than letter-by-letter. Hence, for example New South Wales is filed before Newfoundland.

Locations for maps and illustrations are entered in *italics*, as are titles of books, magazines and newspapers.